"I know there are many people who fall ill when they see this black uniform; we understand that and don't expect that we will be loved by many people." —Heinrich Himmler

"I know there are many that will loath and fear this patch and they should." —Mike Abrams, President WSPMA

The WSPMA patch was worn on the clothing of all members.

If the State were to pay every inmate who served time at the Walls (Washington State Penitentiary) from 1970 to 1980 a $1,000,000, that would be insufficient compensation for the torture they had to endure. No crime committed justified the conditions imposed by the state at that institution. —James Spalding, Director of Corrections

Walls of Secrecy

Stories of Prison Life 1971-1981

How Politicians Turned a Correctional Institution
Into the Top Drug-Trafficking, Gang-Controlled,
Murder Capitol of Washington State

Kelley D. Messinger

(Cell mate to Jim Fogle, author of *Drugstore Cowboy*)

with Emily Lauritzen Waters

Walls of Secrecy: Stories of Prison Life 1971-1981
Copyright 2019 Kelley D. Messinger
All rights reserved.

Book design: Gray Dog Press

ISBN: 978-0-578-55291-0

Printed in the United States of America

Ed. Rev. 020321

Acknowledgments

I would like to credit Don Dodd, who worked at the penitentiary while I was there. With his permission I have included information from his Facebook blog, "Lt. D Dodd Washington State Penitentiary 1970-2000" which you can find at: https://www.facebook.com/groups/1676776052934078/?ref-group_header

I would like to thank James Spalding for all the help he gave me, pictures, and moral support. After getting out of prison, every time I would see Jim the first thing he would ask is, "Are you going to write that book?"

I found the facts and research in Chris Murray's book, *Unusual Punishment*, to be informative and useful. If you enjoyed *Walls of Secrecy*, you must also read *Unusual Punishment*.

Special thanks to the Hoffman family for allowing me to use some of Ethan Hoffman's great pictures from *Concrete Mama*.

I would like to thank John McCoy of *Concrete Mama* for all the help he has given me. If you get a chance to hear John talk on the subject of the Washington State Penitentiary you will find it interesting and disturbing. He will cover a time in corrections that must not be forgotten.

Walls of Secrecy is dedicated to all those inmates who endured constant torture and the many who lost their lives during the State of Washington's great penal experiment.

Special thanks to Dick Morgan, Secretary of Corrections, State of Washington who allowed me to tour correctional facilities throughout the state of Washington.

1980 August

I went to a parole hearing after having completed 10 years on my life sentence and was informed by the board that I would have to do at least another 20 years before they would consider releasing me.

When I got back to my cell I prayed to the Lord. "Lord what do I have to do to get out of here."

A small voice whispered, "Don't worry you will be out soon."

1980 October

The warden informed me that Governor Ray had ordered me released.

Contents

Foreword

In 2016 while serving as Secretary for the Washington State Department of Corrections a Mr. Kelley Messinger wrote to me requesting to interview me for a book he was writing. An ex-con from the bad ol' days of the Penitentiary, I had known Kelley when I was an Officer and later Sergeant at the Penitentiary. This was a time period that resulted in Federal Court ruling the Penitentiary was unconstitutional due to its violence and deplorable conditions of confinement. Kelley was a member of a prison gang known as the "bikers" during the '70s. Not only was he a member of a notorious gang, he was also doing time for a murder committed in my hometown of Walla Walla.

I couldn't imagine a convict[1] from the Concrete Mama[2] era writing an honest account of events but was curious none-the-less. When he arrived at my office, I met a man that struck me as old—he was about my age but it always surprises me when I meet someone I haven't seen since they worked or did time from the '70s. Kelley brought me up to speed on his time since leaving prison and found him to be a well-spoken successful businessman. We spent about two hours together revisiting the most infamous history of the Penitentiary.

---

1 In prison context, the word convict is a honorable title for those who lived by the convict code while demanding the same of their peers (by force if necessary). Official titles of "resident," "inmate," "offender," etc. were considered derogatory by convicts.
2 An excellent photojournalistic book that gave the Penitentiary its dubious nickname: *Concrete mama: Prison profiles from Walla Walla* photographs by Ethan Hoffman; text by John McCoy; foreword by Tom Wicker. Publisher: University of Missouri Press (1981) ISBN: 082620340X

Kelley's tenure at the Penitentiary was a time prisoner wellbeing (and even survival) was determined entirely by prisoners, not staff. All prisons, then and now, are chock full of people with poor decision-making ability and low impulse control. Not to mention only a few years earlier our society had dismantled institutional mental health. Prisons were in transition to become the warehouses for the spontaneously violent mentally ill. Consider that Kelley lived twenty-four hours a day among them. He fell asleep every night locked in a cell with three criminals who all shared those poor decision and low impulse control potentials. He navigated a complex society of criminal gangs constantly maneuvering for power and control over each other.

I've often been asked to tell the stories of when prisoners were in charge of running the prison. It isn't unusual for the stunned audience to respond with "You should write a book." My response has always been "No one would ever believe it." Kelley Messinger has done what I could never do. He has written about that bizarre world from the perspective of a convict in social and confrontational situations staff like me never experienced.

That is not to say *Walls of Secrecy* ignores staff experiences during that period. Kelley relied on one of the Penitentiary's most famous staff to provide some staff perspective. Now retired, Lieutenant Don Dodd was and is respected by both staff and prisoners. This respect was derived from his consistent stand on demanding fairness and delivering decisions that always made things safer for all. He didn't mince words or require a lot of time to make a decision. Anyone wanting anything from Lt. Dodd knew tactics of bluster, whining, or intimidation were a waste of time.

Walls of Secrecy is a work providing a personal insight I have not encountered before. It is a first and rare take on the events of prison reform gone horribly wrong. I hope you find this fascinating as I did.

—Dick Morgan, Secretary for the
Washington State Department of Corrections (Ret.)

Warden James Spalding: Tell me Parley, what problems do you take home with you every night?

Correctional Office Parley Edwards: Only one. The guilt I have for not being able to protect them or the staff.

Parley Edwards. Photo taken by: Ethan Hoffman

Opened in 1887, the Washington State Penitentiary houses the state's worst and most chronic offenders. The main prison compound covers twenty acres.

Photo by Ethan Hoffman. Showing "New" water tower and current configuration of the prison.

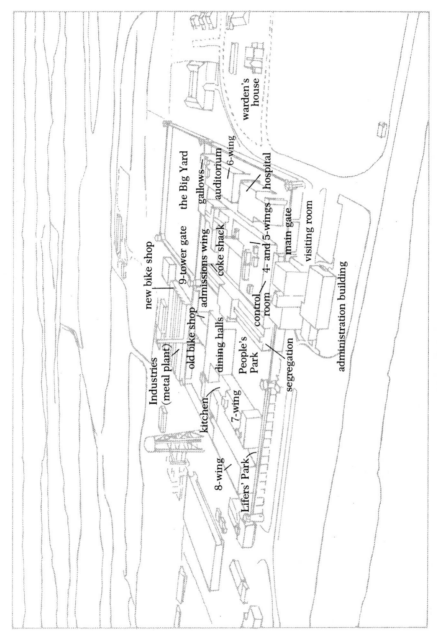

Industries (metal plant)

new bike shop

9-tower gate

the Big Yard

gallows

auditorium

6-wing

old bike shop

admissions wing

coke shack

hospital

dining halls

People's Park

control room

4- and 5-wings

main gate

kitchen

7-wing

segregation

visiting room

8-wing

Lifers' Park

administration building

warden's house

Photo by Ethan Hoffman.

Riding the Big Yard at the walls in Walla Walla.
Photo by Ethan Hoffman.

The Walls of Secrecy

Prelude

One night in 1972, while serving a life sentence, Arthur St. Peter left maximum security at Washington State Penitentiary. He left, not as an escapist, but under the full say-so of the administration. You see, St. Peter had permission to eat dinner in the community under the prison's "take a lifer to dinner" program.

St. Peter excused himself to use the bathroom during dinner. He then climbed out a bathroom window to freedom . . . and his criminal ways. Seven days later he moseyed into a pawn shop. Using a .38 pistol that he'd brought with him from prison, he robbed the shop, shooting both owners, a husband and wife, in the process. The husband died while the wife managed to shoot St. Peter before he left. Later St. Peter was re-arrested when he was caught sitting in his getaway car. He was too badly injured to drive away.

Why was St. Peter, ineligible even for parole, one whom had shown himself to be an agile and determined escape artist, been allowed to leave the prison for dinner? Why did he have access to a gun while in prison? How did he manage to leave the prison for a dinner with local citizens while carrying that gun? You might be asking yourself, "What kind of prison does business that way???"

It is hard for even me to believe it, but this is the prison I lived in for a decade, and St. Peter was one of my friends. This is my story of imprisonment and survival.

My name is Kelley D. Messinger. Under some mind-bending circumstance (I'll describe in more detail later), I served ten years in maximum security at Washington State Penitentiary in the 1970s. While there I adapted to a whole new set of life rules. I learned what it takes for people to live together in confinement, what does and doesn't work under those circumstances. It was a million-dollar experience that I wouldn't ever pay a penny to have.

The things that stay with me, that I think about when I'm alone and my thoughts are free, are the people. Almost fifty years later I can't forget those people, some of whom are still in prison. People that were very good and some that were mostly bad. All of them bring unique, and in some strange way, treasured memories of my prison experience. But first you have to know how I got there.

1

County Lock-up

On December 11, 1970, I stood in a county jail cell as the steel gates slammed shut, a solid, metallic clang ringing as my freedom fled, seemingly forever. I remember my disbelief over the prior five months culminating, hardening into a cold reality at that moment. Over the investigation my thoughts ranged from arrogant insistence that my innocence would be proven, then to depression and disbelief as the investigation ground on, and finally despondency as I sat in that jail cell.

Since my wife Pam's death, it became clear to me that investigators thought I was the killer, but I couldn't believe that the prosecutors would eventually convince a jury. This last part took a while to sink in for me. I had always been taught that the innocent had nothing to fear and that justice would prevail. Little did I know that the investigation, trial and conviction were only the beginning of my mind-altering journey as subject of a most unusual human experiment, where the sane was insane and the moral was immoral, where one lived in an alternate reality that violated any sense of normalcy or decency experienced in the outside world. My mind struggled to grasp what had happened, as well as what was in store, as I made this county jail my home for the next eleven months.

I met Pam in the summer of 1967 before shipping out to southeast Asia, on route to Vietnam. I was 20 years old, serving in the Navy. She was young (17 years old, I thought, though I later learned she was younger than that). We married on May 13, 1968 in Walla Walla, Washington at the county courthouse and I shipped back overseas in June.

From the beginning our marriage was rocky, which shouldn't be a surprise given our youth and the chaotic time we were living in. After I got back from Vietnam in September 1968, I worked at Smith's Frozen Foods in Milton-Freewater, Oregon. In February 1969, I began working for the U.S. Postal Service as a letter carrier, and we moved into a new house the end of July 1970.

By this time Pam had started dating another guy, and I filed for divorce July 1970, the same month we moved into the new house. On August 6, 1970, Pam died.

Earlier that evening Pam left our house at 6:30, heading to a girlfriend's house. I met her later at the Red Apple Restaurant and the two of us took the kids to a babysitter. We drove around for a while and then I went home and went to bed fairly early. Pam said that she was going to sleep out in the car when she got home, waiting for the cats to return. The cats disappeared after we moved in and she hoped they would return. She wasn't there when I got up the next morning, so I put the kids in the car and went looking for her. I checked the Red Apple Restaurant and her girlfriend's house. I didn't find her.

I had to go to work, so I called Pam's mom to see if she would watch the kids; she said that she couldn't because she had other plans. I called in an excuse to work and continued to wonder where Pam might be and what I could do to find her. By this time, I began to wonder if she had been hurt, because it wasn't like her to be gone this long without word. I called the hospital and the police, but I didn't learn anything. Later in the day the Sheriff's office called and wanted to talk to me.

The cold, unvarnished truth was that Pam's body was discovered early in the morning on August 7, 1970, 10 miles away, on a secondary farm road in the middle of a wheat field. Her body told investigators that she died of suffocation, with few other signs of physical violence. Pam's 135-pound, 5'6" body was naked in the field. The crime scene, which I never saw but about which I read and heard extensively during the trial and appeals, was a field of uncut wheat. The Walla Walla County Coroner Henry Lieberman, who was the former Walla Walla Police Department Captain and not a physician, testified at trial that it appeared that Pam's body had been dropped from a helicopter; the crops were undisturbed on all sides of her body. Sheriff deputies later testified that, as they were investigating, they found it impossible to examine the body or crime scene without disturbing the wheat. There were freshly discarded Olympia beer cans alongside of the road, across from Pam's body. Pam's underwear was recovered along the road leading to the field where her body lay.

Of course, I didn't know any of this when the sheriff office first called. When the call came and they said they wanted me to come down and talk to them, I was happy to meet with them, anxious to learn where Pam was. I went to their office to talk. At first, they didn't tell me that Pam's body had been found, but simply asked questions about where I had been the previous night and whether there were problems between me and Pam. I told them that we'd filed for divorce and that Pam had been talking about going to Spokane with her boyfriend. I was questioned for three to four hours and sometime before the middle of the interview investigators told me that Pam was dead. They said her body was found in an uncut wheat field. I signed a consent so investigators could search the house.

The next day they searched the house a second time, again with my consent. I had nothing to hide, I didn't kill her. Besides, I didn't feel that I could deny the search when they told me that they already had a search warrant. Later I learned that the warrant was signed after the search took place, making their false words that gained my consent a violation of my constitutional rights.

Investigators took the contents of the fireplace, which included some of Pam's charred clothes, and the pillows off the bed. Pam's clothes had ended up in the fireplace because the dryer that had come with the house had set them on fire, and the fireplace was the only logical place to put the burning clothes. Regardless of the absurdity of having charred clothes in the fireplace, the clothing found and collected as evidence was not the same clothing as Pam had been wearing, as testified by any and all witnesses in the trial. Investigators also vacuumed the car. One thing they didn't process as evidence were the beer cans found across the street from the body. An investigator at the crime scene remarked that since the husband was Mormon and didn't drink, there was no point in processing the beer cans for fingerprint evidence.

The sheriff office questioned me August 7 and 8, and then I was interviewed twice more in the next couple of months. During these interviews I was repeatedly told that if I was innocent, I had nothing to worry about. Meanwhile, it was increasingly obvious to me that I was the primary target of the investigation. During the last interview the investigating officer said this didn't look like a murder, but more like an accident, similar to one that had occurred several years prior when a pig farmer accidently backed his truck over his wife. He also said that I could plead guilty to manslaughter and have the sentence then set aside, keeping my job with the US Postal Service, as well as collecting the life insurance money. My reply was that if I told that lie, her murderer would go free and I would also have to lie under oath, two eventualities that I was not willing to live with. I was still working at the post office when I was arrested on December 11, 1970.

I got an anonymous call earlier that day that I was going to be arrested. I had worked a full day and then came home and, with the kids at my Mom and Dad's house, I went to my friend Jerry Dubey's gas station, which is where I was arrested. That is when I was booked into the Walla Walla County Jail.

2

The Dark Side of Incarceration

All told I was in the county jail for over a year, and right away I faced a test. Jack Rodriguez, who on the outside lived with his 80-year-old mother, was in jail on murder charges. One night Jack was in the bar drinking too much when he got into an argument with a guy. The guy told Jack that he was coming over to Jack's house later to beat him up after he left the bar. Jack went home, locked the door and got his pistol. Sure enough, the guy showed up and kicked the door open, where Jack and his 80-year-old mother lived.

Jack shot the guy dead and called the police. The police showed up and much to Jack's surprise, arrested him on a murder charge. The police considered the threats made during the barroom argument as premeditation. Jack pled "not guilty," but was found guilty of manslaughter and sent to Washington State Penitentiary in Walla Walla, "Walla Walla" as we called it, to serve his prison sentence.

While Jack was sitting in county jail, waiting for a bus ride to the prison, he had easy access to all the other prisoners. At that prison all the cell doors were welded open so that the prisoners could get to the toilet, which was mounted in the center of the tier. Jack had complete access to other inmates, and they would perform favors for him, regardless of whether they wanted to. Jack was quite fond of a young dentist's kid who was in for a marijuana charge, which was a 20-year felony at the time. One day the kid told his parents in front of everyone that he was being used like a woman. The parents' tough love stopped right there, and he was bailed out of county jail immediately.

Jack thought I could fill in as replacement for the dentist's kid, and I saw this coming. I made it really clear that there was no chance of that happening. However, soon Jack came to me with a shank in his hand, talking about how I better come into his cell. He kept coming toward me as I walked backward toward the rear of the cell block, with my fists up, ready to fight.

As I reached the end of the tier, Jack stepped in thinking that I was trapped and he would have his way with me. Instead, I slammed my foot across his kneecap, dropping him to the floor, which was a trick I learned in Jungle Survival School during Vietnam. I knew that when someone gets kicked in the knee hard, they will always drop their weapon.

I snatched the shank and was going to make him a one-eyed Jack and told him he could choose which eye he wanted to keep. He started pleading, telling me he was just testing me, and he would never have followed through with it. I told him to remember that just two years prior, I had been in Vietnam killing people, and I was not afraid of dying or killing. After that we got along just fine, and when we got to Walla Walla, he told other prisoners that I was a stand-up guy. Maybe he included that I knew how to take care of myself.

To defend me, my parents hired a well-known criminal defense attorney named Herbert H. Friese, who was also a Washington state senator. In spite of my eventual conviction, I felt Mr. Friese did a competent job in my defense. The prosecution's evidence was damning and prejudicial, many would argue unconstitutional. As examples, the prosecution argued that my not testifying at trial implicated me. This violated my 5th amendment right against self-incrimination. Additionally, evidence was raised regarding my relationship with Pam's sister, which was only tangentially relevant to the trial and probably unfairly prejudicial. This further darkened the jury's opinion of me. Then there were the quirky facts raised that I simply couldn't fully explain, like the charred clothing in the fireplace and my not having an alibi on the evening Pam was killed.

On the night of her murder, Pam had a date scheduled with Philip Daniels, an older guy I knew who lived in Walla Walla. Philip was a local EMT and I knew him to be one of Pam's boyfriends. He told his friends that if they wanted easy sex, they should take Pam out. At trial Philip testified that, though they had made the date, he didn't keep it and he hadn't been with Pam that night. Nine years later a mutual friend stated in a sworn affidavit that he knew Philip had in fact kept the date that night with Pam[3]. Apparently, all evidence satisfied the jury in their quest to find me guilty beyond reasonable doubt. They deliberated just six hours, reaching a unanimous agreement of guilty for first-degree murder.

But this book isn't about the trial or my conviction, or even to satisfy the reader regarding my innocence. My mind is perfectly at peace that I had no part in Pam's death and I don't feel compelled to try and erase doubt for those eager to judge me guilty of that crime. Rather this is a book about bare survival during my decade in maximum security under a prison system that could be described nothing short of cruel and unusual. Indeed, that confinement in Walla Walla, the 9th Circuit Court would later rule, was cruel and unusual punishment[4]. During the 1970s, a decade ending with the riot of July 1979, the Washington State Penitentiary was the most violent prison in the US as determined by several different metrics. The sentence imposed on me by the court was a punishment through confinement. But the real punishment I suffered was having to learn to live in a system of experimental, inconsistent administration, as well as violent and deadly gang governance. All of this shaped a dark, terrifying, surreal decade of my life.

---

3 During appeals this information was given to the Washington Court of Appeals. They found it interesting, but wanted more in order for it to make a difference in my case . . . and I didn't have any more information. In the end, this didn't help me.
4 Hoptowit v. Ray, 753 P.2d 779, 784 (9th Cir. 1985).

3

Tried by a Jury of my Peers

After I was taken into custody after trial in December 1971, I was sent first to the state prison in Shelton for two months for classification. I finally entered Walla Walla in February 1972.

What made my prison experience unique was the recent change in prison rules and structure. In the mid-1960s, Washington hired Dr. William R. Conte, known to most as Connie. Connie was a psychiatrist and headed Washington's Department of Institutions, Division of Mental Health. His suggestions helped deinstitutionalize the state's mental health facilities, saving millions of dollars and thus earned him lots of respect from Washington's administrators and legislators. Never mind the fact that those mentally ill people just ended up in another institution: the prisons. In the late 1960s Connie was made Director of Institutions, where he began to make reforms in another division within the Department of Institutions: Division of Adult Corrections.[5]

Before this, Walla Walla was like any other state penitentiary; those in super-custody lived in cells with limited movement, and had limited access to areas of the prison and other prisoners. There was little opportunity for self-expression: all inmates wore identical clothes, had similar haircuts and lived in cells without signs of individuality.

Their lives were well-regulated, with laundry collection handled in an orderly manner, meals served in a regimented style, and inmate counts documented and tracked throughout the day[6]. The downside was

---

5 Murray at 16-18.
6 Murray at 3-11.

boredom and stultifying monotony, while the upside was security and comforting predictability; each day was fairly similar, for better or worse, though things were about to change.

Connie learned through his professional training that criminal behaviors could be changed through a social psychiatric approach. To him this meant "us[ing] anybody that you can find, anywhere, who has the capacity and the willingness to give something of himself in the way of communication to an individual[7]." Whatever that means, Connie knew that to enact his vision of reform, he needed to enlist Washington's long-standing and well-respected superintendent B.J. Rhay.

Rhay had been warden at Walla Walla for fourteen years, and his reign was marked by predictable prison routines[8] under the con-boss system. Under that system, Rhay's authority was unquestioned and absolute. Now, with Connie's suggested reforms, things changed significantly. Maybe Rhay anticipated this weakening of his authority and, as a result, resisted the change. In the end, Rhay probably saw that Connie's ideas were taking hold as part of a larger social trend and the move to Connie's way of thinking was inevitable. Whatever it was, Rhay's authority as warden changed dramatically over the next years[9] [10].

After lengthy discussion and debate, as well as securing funds, Rhay went to Europe for a tour of their prisons in April 1970. The purpose of this tour was to educate Rhay on alternative, yet effective, European prison systems. Rhay traveled to England, France, Holland, Denmark, Norway and Sweden. He found systems that didn't censor prisoner mail. They allowed visitors to freely meet prisoners at their jobs, in their cells and other places in the prison. They even allowed prisoners weekend furloughs. Most importantly, all these policy changes were being pushed through by prisoners, for other prisoners. In a nutshell, these European countries had democratized their prisons.[11]

---

7 Murray at 17.
8 Murray at 12.
9 Murray at 34-36.
10 Murray at 37.
11 Murray at 24-25.

While in Europe, Rhay generally caught vision of what Connie advocated with prisoner self-governance, meanwhile seeing an opportunity to save a lot of money in staffing and other prison costs. In Swedish prisons, guards exercised limited powers; they only made sure inmates don't leave before they'd served their time. Meanwhile Swedish prisoners governed themselves through their councils, enjoying perks like wearing civilian clothes and taking brief trips away from the prison, as well as having money and other things openly sent in by family and friends on the outside.

When prison governance changed, many reforms took hold at the Walla Walla. Before I got there, a protest beginning in December 1970 kicked off, where the prisoners initially just refused shaving and haircuts. It was a peaceable, sit-down strike and, as Rhay tried to resolve the strike and re-balance power, additional inmate demands surfaced. Similar to their European counterparts, inmates wanted freedom from mail censorship and changes in use of segregation and isolation as punishment. They also demanded freedom to work on legal matters and a court to review inmate rules infractions, fewer restrictions on contact with visitors, and better communication with the administration.[12] Basically, they wanted even more say in how the prison was governed.

---

12 Murray at 34.

4

Prison Reforms at Walla Walla

When he got back to Washington, Rhay began what he called "Pride in Culture" programs, where he met with representatives from various ethnic prisoner groups (i.e., blacks, Chicanos and Native Americans). This started the ball rolling toward prisoners organizing into racial and cultural groups, like Black Prisoners Forum Unlimited, Confederated Indian Tribes and United Chicanos, which was a new system of social organization for the prison. Previously the only inmate organizations ran across racial and cultural divides, grouping prisoners into sports teams, a Junior Chamber of Commerce, Jaycees, and Toastmasters.[13]

Prisoners, realizing they had influence, organized protests. Once the protests started, Connie started to respond to letters from prisoners. The balance of power was changing and Connie, in Olympia, was getting into prisoner disputes, though he'd try and deflect them back to Rhay. This forced Rhay to negotiate with protest and strike leaders, where at least one of their demands (no more haircuts and shaving, unless the inmate wanted it) was met.[14] Inmates understood that if Rhay didn't give you what you want, you can just go to Connie in Olympia and he'll respond.

Eventually Rhay offered more inmate freedoms. Inmates could have additional visits (even without a divider on the table), and had fewer restrictions on lights-out and movement through the prison. Critical to these changes was the creation of the Residential Government Counsel (RGC), where each cell block got to elect representatives, as well as have

---

13 Murray at 25-26.
14 Murray 35-36.

their own justice system, including judges, law enforcement officials, and lawyers.

All of this was modeled after the Swedish prison system. Unfortunately, there were vast differences between European prisons, which were much smaller and generally community-based, and huge, high-walled state penitentiaries like Walla Walla. Someone probably should have seen that the existing US penitentiary system was too different from Europe's community-based mini-prisons to successfully adopt much from them. Walla Walla couldn't just initiate a few reforms on prisoner governance and end up with the self-governance system so successful in European mini-prisons, given the huge underlying differences.[15]

---

15 Murray at 97-98.

5

An Idea Gains Momentum

Nonetheless, Connie's ideas had lots of political oxygen and the state forged ahead, trying to mimic the European prisons. The resulting reforms led to more lax security in the prison. Officer shakedowns of prisoners became infrequent, and, with an open visiting room, drugs flowed freely into the prison.* The same month as these changes, there was a violent death in the dressing room of the prison recreation building. Two more deaths followed within four months. This was a remarkable uptick in murder rates: under Rhay's unquestioned authority over the previous decade, there were only three murders. Now, in less than six months under this new power structure, they matched that number.[16]

Another ominous, and certainly related, trend began: prisoners started arming themselves. All three deaths in early 1971 were stabbing deaths. Sometimes knives were smuggled in and sometimes knives were built in the prison shop,[17] and everyone seemed to be packing knives. This trend continued and in 1973, the Walla Walla Union Bulletin reported lots of prison deaths through stabbing. A riot in 1974 resulted in a nurse getting stabbed, as well as a prison guard later that year.*

Once the reforms were set in place and some of the scary, violent consequences surfaced, any guard with sufficient seniority quickly bid on nights, retired, or opted for more secure posts. Most of the guards with

---

* Credit: Blog of Lt. D. Dodd, Washington State Penitentiary, 1970-2000. Note: This and all following references indicated by an asterisk are the same.
16 Murray at 38.
17 Murray at 38.

five years or less quit altogether.* Shortly after the reforms an officer was stabbed six times when he intervened in a fight between inmates. The good news is the officer survived, though he quickly resigned.*

6

"The Law" at Walla Walla

The RGC at Walla Walla was supposed to band together into a loose clique, not really a gang, and decide who was in charge of everything in the prison. One leader would run the kitchen, another the laundry. Every member of each group ideally supported the group's authority in that area. So, in order to get a job in the kitchen, the kitchen leader had to approve it, which usually meant being in that leader's circle of friends.

Unfortunately for Connie, initially Walla Walla prisoners didn't buy into the RGC. At the first RGC election, the only prisoners elected were dings (which is what we called the mentally ill). Connie saw this wasn't going to work and, frustrated, went back to Olympia. After conferring with others, he decided that they would let the prisoners form clubs, who would bridge the gap between the existing con-boss system and the new European system of prisoner self-governance.

As I look at it years later, maybe the idea worked too well, because before you knew it, the prison clubs were in control of the prison. Clubs formed, mostly along racial divides, which would be called gangs today. Each club earned a unique reputation and had distinct membership. As I saw it, Walla Walla had nine major clubs, with a few less noteworthy clubs that came and went.

1. Confederated Tribes for the Indians (CTI): They suffered greatly in prison, though they had a fairly large membership. Their weakness was its members were first loyal to their own Native American tribe, and only loyal to the gang as an afterthought. This meant that if something happened to someone that was

a part of the gang but wasn't part of your same tribe, the gang members might look the other way. They lacked cohesion.

This group was further weakened by a big alcohol problem. One time a rumor got started that if you drained orange shellac (available through the furniture factory) through 3-day-old French bread, it would remove the poisons and make the alcohol safe to drink. This was, of course, wishful thinking, and the rumor left several club members dead and many blinded. This club had a particularly violent relationship with the Chicano Club; many members of both groups were killed through their constant fighting.

2. Chicano Club: If you were of Mexican descent, you could join the Chicanos. At one point, they opened up a cantina, with hard liquor and working ladies available. They were a cohesive group and quick to defend each other, though their constant battles with the CTI led to many member deaths.

3. Lifers with Hope: If you had a life sentence, you could join this club. This is the club that Warden Rhay embraced as a model club, and he gave them lots of perks; some of this group's members got to leave prison from time to time to visit their families and homes. Maybe Rhay favored them because it was the club operated closest to the con-boss system, which was something he was familiar with and believed in. The Lifers with Hope had a large membership base, mostly white. Their purpose was self-help and community service.[18]

4. Gays Club: This was a loosely-held membership, with all members gay. There were several types of gays in prison at the time. The "girls" dressed and acted like girls, wearing dresses, make-up, and feminine hair styles; several even had actual

---

18 Murray at 43.

breasts. The kids were also gays, who looked and acted like straight men, but were willing to be the recipient in sexual encounters. At that time in prison, if you were on the receiving end of a man-to-man sexual encounter, then you were considered gay, though if you were on the delivery side of a man-to-man sexual encounter, then you were considered straight. Pressure punks had no homosexual propensities but would be a kid when threatened or intimidated. No one respected pressure punks.

The Gay Liberation Army was an off-shoot of the Gays Club. They were blamed for several murders and even some bomb-building, and that gave them some tough-guy credentials in the prison. In spite of this, they still had to be cautious in the main population.

5. Alcoholics Anonymous: This group obviously took its name and identity from the non-prison group, though in prison they were involved in drug running, murders, and pruno (alcohol brewed by and for prisoners) production.

6. Washington State Penitentiary Automobile Association (WSPAA): As its name suggests, the members shared an interest in cars and built custom cars, often expert-quality. This group had a tendency to get into wars with the AA members, and several car club members were killed, until eventually the WSPAA disbanded, leaving their paint booth to the Bike Shop.

7. Black Prisoners Forum Unlimited (BPFU): If you were black, you could join this club. It was by far the largest club in the prison, which numbers gave them a lot of power. Most members lived in six wing, and a fair number lived in eight wing, until they got into a war with the Bike Shop. After that the eight wing club members mostly migrated to six wing.

8. Born Again Christians: This group had a reputation as being the chosen club for sex offenders. It never accumulated much power.

9. Washington State Penitentiary Motorcycle Association (WSPMA): I knew the most about this club because, after a couple of years, I was part of it. To join you needed to have an interest in the motorcycling lifestyle. You had to be invited to join, and then you had to prospect for three months, which was a sort of initiation period to see if you were a good fit for the club. A prospect had to do whatever a member asked, though the prospect should never be asked to do something the asking member would not do himself. If you belonged to an outlaw motorcycle club (e.g., Hell's Angels) on the streets, then you did not have to prospect. I considered this club to live Germany's Secret Police (SS or Schutzstaffel) motto: My honor is my loyalty. Our club had occasional wars with other clubs, though in a twelve-year period, only one biker lost his life and only a handful were assaulted. No one seemed to mess with this group for very long. This club started out with about seven founding members, and not much power. Within a year, its membership swelled to between 30 and 60 members, and then leveled-off around 30 members. We were powerful enough to be choosey about our membership and from time to time a member was ousted for excessive drug use or other activities that could hurt the club. At the height of its influence, the Biker's Club controlled the staff, and much of prison activity.

The prison biker's club includes members of the Gypsy Jokers, Hell's Angles, Banditos, and other "outlaw" motorcycle clubs. Rivals on the streets, they claim to be "bros" behind the walls. Photo by Ethan Hoffman

Within a year these clubs controlled the prison. Your club was your family, with members often willing to die for one another. If you messed with a club member, then you were prepared to take on the entire club membership, though the clubs varied in their cohesiveness.

As the power shifted from administrators to prisoners, the clubhouses became off-limits to prison administration, eventually becoming the exclusive domain of the club's leadership.[19] Meanwhile, clubs started hosting banquets, inside and outside the prison, with hundreds in attendance. This resulted, along with other rule changes, in prisoner access to many perks of the outside world, like drugs and weapons.[20]

19 Murray at 58, 60.
20 Murray at 59.

7

Welcome to Walla Walla

I arrived at Walla Walla in an old Greyhound bus, along with a bunch of other prisoners. We were all bound together, with our handcuffs attached to a chain at our waists, and then we also had leg chains. On the bus ride, some prisoners were singing "Put Your Hand in the Hand of the Man," "I Fought the Law and the Law Won," and other prison songs. In our group were a couple young guys (early 20s, I guessed) both sent to prison on marijuana changes. I was 24 years old and probably about their same age, but I felt older somehow; maybe it was my time in Vietnam and the year with a first-degree murder charge hanging over my head that had made me old before my time.

The bus pulled into the vestibule or sally port (it was between the outer and inner gates) of the prison, called The Walls. My initial impression of prison was that it was absolutely filthy, which surprised me. The area was obviously unmaintained, with rotting trash, peeling paint and grime everywhere. Once we got out of the bus, we had no opportunity to blend in because we all wore coveralls, while the rest of the prisoners wore whatever clothing they had access to. Once we got out of the sally port, we entered the prison itself, in an area later known to me as People's Park. It was a big, outside area and I noticed three campfires burning and at least two cardboard shacks, like what you would see in a homeless camp. The prisoners all seemed to be staring at us, almost as if they'd been waiting for us to get there. I asked, "Why are all these guys standing around here?" A sergeant replied, "Half of these guys are probably here to see you."

A shot of People's Park.
Photo supplied by James Spalding, Director of Corrections.

It surprised me to learn that my reputation preceded me. When I arrived, I was already known as a real tough guy. I was reputed to have nearly escaped when I was at the county jail, but that was a totally undeserved credential. The truth was that there were seven inmates, including myself, waiting for transfer to the Walla Walla. Some of these guys, not including me, decided to try escaping by removing bricks from the back wall. At lock-up time, guards circled back of the tiers which would expose the plan. So, part of the escape plot included making sure that the walk around back didn't occur. On the night of intended escape, the Right Reverend Raby (who was convicted of some kind of fraud) broke into song, and he was honestly a great singer. Then this old, black prisoner joined the show by dancing. This all proved a helpful distraction from the back-tier inspection, as the guards stopped to watch the show without circling to the back of the tiers. Once the show was over, they just moved along. This allowed the brick removal to continue, and the next day the pace accelerated. Eventually a wino serving time tipped off the guards, and the next day the headlines in the Walla Walla Union Bulletin read, "Messinger and Gang Attempt Jail Break." Since no one would testify against anyone else, the charges didn't go anywhere.

I was also supposedly some kind of hard-bitten survivalist, due to my jungle training in Vietnam, which was also based on a pretty loose portrayal of my Vietnam training and service. I had served in Vietnam and been trained in lots of things, but I was always a good, law-abiding service member during my time in the military.

Someone told me that they had heard that I was part of the Weathermen Underground on the outside, which was a radical gang of the 1960s. This was completely untrue as I had never been part of that gang and didn't even know any of its gang members.

Also, Lieutenant Glenn Henderson, a prison guard, told the entire morning shift on the day that I arrived that I was an extreme escape risk, had bomb-building skills, was a highly-decorated Vietnam veteran with experience in Naval Intelligence, and had ties with radical outside groups. Aside from having a secret clearance in the Navy, the same level of security clearance of virtually all service members, this was all fiction.

Finally, my criminal conviction was for first-degree murder of my wife. I guess conviction for this violent, cold-hearted crime served to cement my reputation as a real badass. I think back to that characterization and find it ridiculous, though that reputation really did protect me while in prison.

After going through People's Park, they took us to the property room, where we were supposed to be fingerprinted. On one occasion while running late and in a hurry the Lt in charge forgot to take fingerprints of one of the inmates so not wanting to have to admit the mistake he submitted his own fingerprints. The FBI later questioned these prints since they did not match their records. Once we were processed, we were taken to four wing, or fish wing as we called it. We all started out in single-man cells in four wing and to get there we had to go the entire length of Blood Alley.

Blood Alley got its name because of the prodigious amount of blood spilt there. This area was a high-traffic area leading to Four, Five and Six Wings, as well as the prison auditorium, the side door of the hospital, and the BPFU clubhouse. This walkway was lined with either chain link fence or tall buildings on both sides and was a covered sidewalk with a hump in the middle, so that someone standing on one end of the walkway couldn't see to the other end of the walkway. All of this created a free area for prisoner violence, because neither guard nor prisoner could see what happened on Blood Alley by watching from the towers, the wall, or even the other end of the walkway.[21]

Since we arrived, the two young guys there on marijuana charges were being jeered at and had a lot of cat calls directed toward them. Some prisoners were yelling that those two were going to be their bitches. As we went through People's Park, one prisoner came up and slapped the one guy on the ass and gave him a big hug. This poor guy literally peed himself, which increased the hooting and hollering. A guard walked us part-way down Blood Alley, stopped and then pointed further down saying, It's down there, second door on the left. As we passed what I came to know as the BPFU clubhouse, one of the young guys was forced into the clubhouse. I understood later that he was repeatedly (about a dozen times) raped or sexually assaulted. This guy ended up being what we called a pressure punk. Unfortunately, it was difficult to overcome a reputation as a pressure punk; you had to get a knife and stab or kill another prisoner to show that you weren't free game anymore.

This was my introduction to prison life. Quickly I picked up a few basic rules:

1. Stay away from drugs. This was a lot harder than it sounds, given the unique structure of prison. Most of the prison population (I estimate 80%) had two common background characteristics: 1. No father in their lives while they were growing up; and 2. Drug use. As a result, most of the prisoners spent every day searching for drugs, and most would do anything to get the drugs. Prisoners who got regular visits were told that their visitors needed to bring in drugs to share or suffer the violent consequences. As a result, even if you didn't do drugs, you could be forced into the drug trade. At that time, staff was bringing in most of the drugs because the consequences for them were pretty

21 Murray at 122.

minor and the reward pretty lucrative. If caught, a guard would lose his job and that was all. While dealing drugs, a prison guard could easily multiply his salary by three or four.

2. Don't owe money. I knew one guy who was killed over a 50-cent debt. I learned that once the debtor dies, the debt is never repaid. Therefore, it is better to just get rid of a small debtor, if one is looking to send a message about debt defaults. This message was very effective in getting debtors to pay on-time.

3. Stay away from the homosexuals. Like the drug wars, you risked finding yourself at odds with someone you'd rather not cross. But, like staying away from drugs, this was more difficult than it sounds. Pressure punks might have to decide between giving sex or getting a money order sent to another prisoner's account.

Obviously, another rule was you never wanted to violate was being caught ratting on someone. Rats were either dead or in protective custody in very short order. Of course, avoiding the label of snitch sometimes involved stepping over or around a dead body, stop[ping] his ears to cries for help, or ignor[ing] the bloody hands of perpetrators as they fled the scene of a crime. It wasn't callousness; it was self-preservation. Being witness to a murder was danger enough. Assisting a dying man meant you were on his side, and that meant you might be killed as well. For the worst of the worst, there wasn't much humanity to lose, but feigned indifference to the suffering of others diminished each man every time he turned away.[22]

In September 1970 a man named Donald Dodd began work at Washington State Prison as a correctional officer, and he stayed for 30 years. We came to know one another, though we were on different sides of the table. In writing my story I used his also, which he shared with me through his blog. His memories show the prison's dysfunction during the 1970s, from another angle.

---

22 Murray pp. 154-55.

8

Finding My Place

I stayed in four wing for a year. My first job was clerk in the control room, where I typed memos, letters and forms. I think I got this assignment because the prison staff wanted me in a job where they could keep an eye on me. I was paid $5 a month, which was one of the better-paying jobs in the prison. Eventually I moved to the industrial area, where I started out as a janitor, but quickly became an electrician, and then the prison's emergency electrician. It was there that I met James Fogle, who was a prisoner working as a machinist. We got on great and eventually Jim invited me to live in six wing in a 4-bed cell with him and another guy named David Riel. Interestingly David Riel and James Fogle were co-conspirators in the crime that resulted in their prison sentence . . . and now they were prison cellmates. I didn't formally join a club for three years and for that time, Dave and Jim served as my prison family.

While Jim Fogle was living in six wing, he wrote the best-selling book *Drug Store Cowboy*, which was later made into a movie. The book focused on the crimes Jim and Dave committed while in Walla Walla County, prior to returning to prison. Jim told me one time that serving time in prison was his job and his vacations were when he was released and back robbing drug stores. He even served time in San Quentin, and he often compared the two. "This joint here is way more dangerous than San Quentin," he'd say, even though he'd been stabbed in San Quentin over a one-eyed Filipino girl.

Since this was my first prison experience, I wasn't a very good judge of how dangerous it was. I later learned that compared to Attica or the New Mexico State Penitentiary, the Washington State Penitentiary wasn't really that bad, if you just looked at inmate murders. As an example, from 1970 to 1981, there were only 29 murders at Walla Walla reported, whereas in Attica in one day 43 people died in 1971. However, that statistic about being only 29 murders in that decade didn't include lots of deaths wrongly classified as suicides[23], or results of really poor medical care.[24]

At the time prisoners could go to the assignment lieutenant and give him names of prisoners wanting to live together. As long as all the prisoners agreed, the assignment lieutenant went along with it. This led to prisoners fixing up cells, then retaining a sort of ownership of the cell and actually charging rent to others living in the cell.[25] So when a prisoner suggested a living arrangement, as agreed by the potential cellmates, the lieutenant checked with the owner of the cell before making the assignment. This meant that the renter needed to pay the "owner" rent, or risk getting seriously hurt. During Associate Superintendent Jim Harvey's first year (August 1974 to August 1975), the process of cell assignment changed, and prisoner suggestions of cell assignments weren't honored by the administration. When Harvey stopped letting prisoners control their own cell assignments, this real estate rental enterprise evaporated, and some prisoners weren't happy about it.

Lifers with Hope, Warden Rhay's favorite club, was the first club to stake ownership on a piece of prison real estate. As early as April 1971, Lifers with Hope declared a grassy land between seven and eight wings as their own, building a brick-paved walkway, complete with an arched bridge spanning a fishpond. They grew flowers and shrubs and later added picnic tables. At one end of their park they claimed a former clothing room as their clubhouse.[26] Other clubs followed suit, and soon most clubs had clubhouses and other places they could call their own. Rhay

---

23 Murray at 157.
24 Murray at 106. In the mental health unit was known for a number of suicides in which the deceased was found hung, with his hands tied behind his back. One person described Dr. Hunter's 3rd floor mental health ward as "a complete nightmarish torture chamber." *Id.* At 102.
25 Murray at 95.
26 Murray at 44.

responded shortly by changing the name to People's Park and made the RGC responsible for regulating its use[27].

Other prison property was also under private ownership. A good example was tables in the chow hall. All tables sat four and were bolted to the floor. Prisoners could buy or rent a table, or just eat standing along the wall. Guards would not allow you to eat sitting on the floor, and you were always cautious of a kind stranger inviting you to sit at his table; in prison, nothing was free.

Everyone knew everyone else's business and there was a loose hierarchy among prisoners, based on their crime. Burglars were considered neither good nor bad, but really run of the mill. Armed robbery was a violent enough crime that it drew respect. Child molesters were generally treated badly, though I knew one guy, a plumber in the prison who had access to lots of plumbing fixtures if you were remodeling your cell (porcelain was much preferred over the standard epoxy sinks). Before prison, this plumber picked up a couple of runway teenage boys and bought them milkshakes, with expectation of something in return. One of the boys spilled a milkshake in the truck and wouldn't clean it up. The plumber drove them off the highway and then parked under a bridge, took out a knife, forced them both to take off their clothes, and raped them. In his words, "I took both of them and had my f___ing way with them." Even though he was serving time for child molesting, he was considered an alright guy because, in his words, "the little punks showed no respect." Even though he was a child molester, his was the kind of violent crime that earned the other prisoners' respect. The plumber also had a powerful drug connection, and this probably helped ensure his safety while in prison.

After my arrival at the prison, I took a while to consider my club options. While the BPFU was powerful, I wasn't black and so I couldn't join. Besides, what went on inside that clubhouse was pretty depraved.[28]

---

27 Murray at 44.
28 "[T]he club's meeting place was carved into a warren of little rooms. There were shooting galleries, gambling tables, and rooms for homosexual activity. And not all the sex was consensual. Some of the more predatory blacks would pick a younger, weaker inmate as he arrived at the penitentiary and claim him as their own. Some of these

Eventually I found various ways to cozy up to the Biker's Club. I would pass on bits of information that were useful to them. I also would make or lay access to bike parts they needed. After about 3 years, I was invited as a member without going through the normal prospecting period. Various favors to the group had sufficiently proven my loyalty, I guessed.

---

inmates were made to dance naked atop a table and then be sold in a single night to six, eight, or ten men for their sexual pleasure." Murray at 90.

9

Perks of Self-Government

Soon after creation, clubs started hosting banquets where they could invite speakers from the outside. The Confederated Indian Tribes were first, and other clubs soon followed. Prison rule reforms first involved curbing censorship of outgoing mail, through policy crafted by the RGC. Once all these reforms started rolling in mid-1971, Connie resigned. It was an abrupt resignation, which he explained a decade later as the result of his frustration with state administrative reorganization and labor union control.[29] His resignation was followed by some stop-gap appointments, but basically for the next two years, Rhay was on his own and he worked hard to institute the reforms suggested by Connie.[30]

From the start, these reforms made things more dangerous for everyone. Not only did violence inside the prison increase, but the whole community was put in danger. A prime example of this was St. Peter. St. Peter was an old convict, as evidenced by his inmate number that began with a "0". He was about 5'2" and weighed maybe 100 pounds. Lieutenant Dodd remembers watching him run around the big yard with his legs tied together by a piece of string 22 inches in length; apparently St. Peter was practicing running while wearing leg irons.* When he was away from the prison for a "take a Lifer to dinner" occasion in April 1972, St. Peter used a trip to the bathroom to escape, climbing out the bathroom window. Before he was arrested, he managed to rob a pawn shop, meanwhile killing the pawn shop's owner and wounding the owner's wife.* When he left

---

29   Murray at 47.
30   Murray at 48.

the prison for dinner that night he took from the prison his .357 Tiger pistol, which he used in his crime. The pawn shop owner and his wife managed to shoot and wound St. Peter during the robbery and so when he was arrested, St. Peter was in his escape car, unable to drive away due to his injuries. Later they found a duplicate pistol in the industries area of the prison.* A search of St. Peter's cell (once he returned to prison) found $2000 cash, and a 1975 search of the Lifers clubhouse found two guns, money, binoculars and three hand-held radios, all reportedly belonging to St. Peter.*

Dick Morgan, a guard who eventually rose to be Director of Corrections, remembers the last big escape attempt, which occurred at eight wing. The would-be escapists tunneled out from the Lifer's club by going under the foundation of eight wing, then walking over to the other side of the basement, and again, digging their way out under a second foundation. By the time the escape route was realized, many people were aware of it, including the staff. St. Peter, a very experienced escapist, was the first to emerge from the tunnel, where he met staff waiting with guns drawn. He fell to the ground, pistol in hand, two others took off running and were shot. An experienced libertine like St. Peter should have known better than to join in a widely publicized escape, but by then he was old and desperate. He always told me, Kelley, you should never try to get out if more than four people are involved in the plan.

St. Peter was an annoyance to the prison, determined escapist that he was, and so when the opportunity arose, Superintendent Spaulding transferred St. Peter to a maximum-security facility in Jefferson City, Missouri.* Dodd recalls transporting St. Peter from Jefferson City, Missouri to Walla Walla so he could testify in a murder trial. The plane stopped in Cheyenne, Wyoming for fuel and Dodd noticed St. Peter looking intently at the airport layout as they landed. On the return trip two days later, Dodd instructed the pilot to stop anywhere but Cheyenne for fuel, and so when they landed in Nebraska, St. Peter was upset. Once out of the plane, he asked if he could have his restraints removed so he could stretch, which request Dodd, through smothered chuckles, denied. Dodd always wondered if someone on St. Peter's payroll was waiting for St. Peter's return trip through Cheyenne, Wyoming.* When they searched St. Peter's cell after his first escape attempt, they found $2000.* When St. Peter escaped from Washington State Prison in 1978 he used a tunnel. Having been tipped off about the escape, guards were waiting when he emerged from the tunnel. Guards found St. Peter armed with a .38 pistol.*

10

Life in Six Wing

Six wing was more than half occupied by members of the BPFU, and this group was particularly violent, so while I lived there, special safety measures were in-place. Old cons like Jim Fogle weren't about to leave their long-time cell, already paid for, just because the neighborhood changed, so the left-behinds found ways of ensuring their own safety. When I shared a cell with Fogel, we had a chain to wrap around our door in case something violent happened and the cell block was under siege. Also, in the cell were several broom handles to which shanks could be attached in case someone tried to burn out the cell. These were just some commonsense improvements, necessary for survival.

As far as prisoner weapons at Walla Walla, I don't know what it was like before I got there. But by the time I arrived weapons were found daily throughout the prison. Shanks, prison slang for knives, had blades at least six inches long. Ice pick-type weapons were made from screwdrivers or pitchfork tines with some type of handle. Prisoners also had clubs, which were shortened ax or hammer handles. A sock with a large padlock or rock in the toe could accomplish the same as a club. There were also zip guns, which sounds dangerous, but I don't remember anyone ever being seriously hurt with one. Some prisoners had brass knuckles, which proved fatal in many cases. Not that anyone died from being punched with brass knuckles, but once you used them in a fight, you usually got shanked at some point down the road and the shanking was often fatal. Nunchucks were often found, as well as garrotes made out of thin wire. Spears were usually a broom handle equipped with a shank.

6 Wing cell block. Jim Fogle, author of *Drug Store Cowboy*,
lived on the second tier. (C tier.)
Photo supplied by James Spalding, Director of Corrections

Photo of Walla Walla prison showing locations of the hospital and 6 Wing. Photo supplied by James Spalding, Director of Corrections

The more clever or crafty prisoners came up with other means of hurting their fellow prisoner. There was battery acid in pruno, rat poison in coffee or rubbing alcohol in a drink. Putting Teflon tape in a cigarette could prove fatal, as could putting gasoline in your cell's light bulb. To get gasoline in a light bulb, you drilled a small hole in the bulb and filled it with a very flammable fluid. When the light turned on, the burning fluid showered the room. Sometimes intravenous drugs were laced with rat poison, and sometimes heroin wasn't cut properly, and therefore toxic. Statistics on prisoner deaths don't include these more inventive murder methods, because the deaths were classified as accidents or overdoses. Death resulting from heroin up the anus was always written off as a drug smuggler, whose loaded condom had accidently burst. I know that wasn't always accurate. Also, lots of the "suicides" simply weren't suicides. I remember one prisoner had supposedly slashed both of his wrists— slashed them so brutally that the tendons in both wrists were destroyed. It made me wonder how he slashed them both without working wrists.

Besides the constant danger, which really was everywhere in the prison, and which we were somewhat able to mitigate, the worst thing about six wing was the large number of boom boxes echoing through the cell block at night. That was something not openly permitted, yet it was tolerated by guards, who feared retaliation. When I took over as electrician for the prison engineering department, I had access to the plumbing and electrical tunnel, and it was a simple job to rewire so that we could blow a fuse anytime. When the fuse blew, someone would holler that the boom box was using too much juice and blew the circuit. Easy fix, in my view.

Six wing had three tiers on each side, for a total of six tiers. The higher the tier, the lower the real estate value. Plus, there was constant pressure to relocate to safer wings, with whites opting for eight wing and blacks opting for six wing. Of course, relocating often meant abandoning a cell that you had worked hard to own. Jim Fogle was not one to leave property behind and, being an old con, he had some measure of protection. That, combined with my Bike Shop membership, made our cell off-limits to uninvited prisoners.

Inmates can make something dangerous out of practically anything as this sample from one guard's collection of confiscated weapons shows.
Photo taken by Ethan Hoffman.

When war broke out between the Bike Shop and BPFU over Cannibal's attack of Jimmy, a Bike Shop buddy, cell exoduses picked up speed. Lots of whites moved to eight wing and blacks moved to six wing. This worked pretty well, with both sides sitting down and exchanging cells in a civilized manner. The cell swapping left few hard feelings, with both sides sensing it was a fair exchange of wealth.

11

A Move to Eight Wing

After the war between the Bike Shop and BPFU, I moved to eight wing to be with my Bike Shop brothers. Eight wing had a colorful history as home of several notable riots. With three tiers on each side, there were a total of six tiers. Each cell had four bunks and one toilet and sink. Showers were toward the back of the wing, and the showers resembled, at least in our estimation, German World War II gassing chambers. Clothes were left outside, and it was just a big room with shower nozzles hanging from pipes ten feet above the floor. The water temperature, set by a guard, varied according to the status held by the showering group. Being powerful, Bike Shop members had first priority with a comfortable temperature, as Sergeant Morgan knew that keeping the Bike Shop happy improved dramatically the odds of a peaceful wing.

After the upper tiers of prison hierarchy showered, the steerage class used the shower. This often-included lots of sexual activities for some working ladies. By then the shower reeked of human feces from the prisoners who just used the corners like toilets. The Bike Shop didn't tolerate that sort of behavior during their shower time.

When first walking into eight wing the stench was overwhelming, though it was maybe worse in four or six wings. Hygiene in prison was generally a problem. With no open ventilation, all circulated air originated from dirty fans in the basement, where it was damp and moldy. A dark, musty smell circulated through the cell block, and that was all we got in the way of air. Some enterprising inmates ran a laundry service and they hung clothes to dry in their cells, which only added a dankness to the olfactory mix. Then, in late afternoons, the stench of feces emanating from the showers infused itself into the cell block's soul-sucking, nauseating odor.

The German SS style showers in 8 Wing at the Walls in Walla Walla.
Photo taken by Ethan Hoffman.

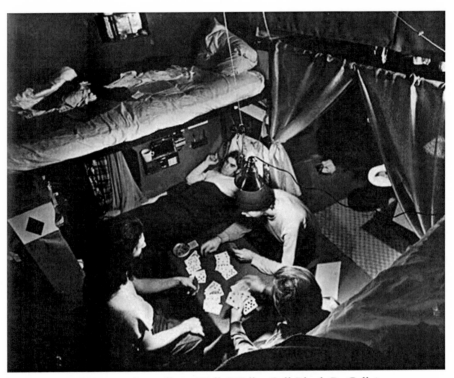

8 Wing at the walls in Walla Walla, Cell Block B, Cell 1.
On the bed, Miss Nancy, under the lamp, her man.
Photo by Ethan Hoffman.

12

The Chow Hall

The chow hall was a huge building, divided by a wall into two dining areas. Tables seated four and were bolted to the floor. Eating utensils were steel, as were the trays. Coffee came from big pots emptied into metal pitchers, where coffee was finally poured into individual cups. Many an inmate was badly burned by a thrown scalding hot pitcher of coffee. This sort of violence made no sense to me. I shortly learned the trays served as effective armor in knife fights, though magazines worked just as well and weren't as bulky.

Each chow hall had two serving areas, so two parallel lines formed down the center of the hall, both peeling off to opposite sides at the steam tables. Inmates ladled food onto your tray and determined your share, based on your position in the prison hierarchy. No one club ran the kitchen, so there were representatives from all the clubs at the service table. Of course, you could ask for an additional portion, but unless you were sufficiently high on the food chain, your request might not be granted. Nothing was free in prison.

I remember Officer Donald Dodd went by the book and was always fair, though he seldom backed down. When he ordered you to stand for a shakedown, you either complied or you fought, because there was no in-between. As a new officer, Dodd was assigned to monitor the steam table in one of the dining halls. The steam table was where food was served, and at the same time kept the food warm, and the serving was done by inmates. So, the officer assigned to the steam table would be up front in the chow hall and was in charge. Right off, Officer Dodd noticed this large, white man sitting at a table right in front of the steam table, and he was staring directly at Dodd, no smiling, just a cold stone stare. When the chow hall emptied out, the new officer asked "Big" Jack Keen, a guard with a lot of experience, what the story with the big white guy was who sat up front giving off death stares. This inmate was Bill Waltman, who was a heavy-weight prizefighter-come prisoner, who they say had sparred with Sonny Liston. "Big" Jack laughed and told Officer Dodd, "He's not getting enough to eat, so we generally just give him a nod when they start closing down the steam table so he can get seconds." After that, if I was not in charge of overseeing the steam table, but working as the acting sergeant in charge of the dining hall, at the rear of the hall I would have Waltman sit back there with me, so I could give him the nod when we closed down the line," said Dodd.

One day Dodd sent a prisoner who cut in line to the end of the line, which set the inmate on a rant about how Dodd was a racist (the inmate was black, and Dodd is white), but the inmate acquiesced. Later that same meal the inmate brought four of his buddies to visit Dodd at his table, and soon Dodd was surrounded by these folks. The inmate and Dodd talked for a bit and then the five returned to their table, with Dodd thinking that he'd sure handled that confrontation well. He turned around and noted that Waltman was standing behind him with his big arms crossing his chest. Waltman then asked Dodd if he needed any help.*

In 1970 the prison had a dairy, five chicken houses, an excellent hog farm and a truck garden, all run by Correctional Industries. Washington's Department of Fish and Game brought truckloads of salmon, and meals cost 87 cents per day, per inmate.* These industries later gave way to a more commercialized food supply.

The preparation section, aka the kitchen where the food storage areas, coolers and freezers were, was separated from the serving area by a wall. The freezers served a dual purpose; along with food preservation they also served as a non-lethal discipline area for errant inmates. An inmate might reconsider his actions after spending, without clothes, two hours in a freezer. It was a rehab center of sorts, an opportunity for a second chance, for some of the wayward ladies, in an environment where adultery carried the death penalty. It sounds harsh, but two numbingly cold hours beats lying dead on a sidewalk.

Everything in the kitchen had a price. Wedding cake was available, for a certain cost. A picnic lunch for the big yard wasn't a problem, if the price was right. Snacks for cells weren't an issue, if you paid the price. Whoever controlled the kitchen could make a lot of extra money, and he usually did. In hindsight, there is little wonder why people got killed over who ran the kitchen.

The kitchen was absolutely filthy. It was never inspected by the staff, who all understood the injury likely resulting for interference with kitchen operations. Along all the walls was a gray stain on the concrete floor about six inches wide due to rodent urine. The kitchen was infested with rodents. Of course, the prison used rodent poison, but because the poison served as a means of getting high (or really sick, depending on the dosage), it was traded among prisoners.

Another perk of working in the kitchen was holding parties there at night, where guards were not permitted to enter. One of the coolers was a bedroom for couples, or they could sneak away to the basement. Lots of pruno was available. Inmates always made two trash cans of pruno: one for the guards to find and show their bosses so that they knew the guards were doing their jobs, and one for the prisoners to market, sell and drink by the cup, quart or gallon. Peach pruno was the good stuff, though canned fruit was high dollar. Pruno made of split peas was the cheapest stuff. Pruno was easy to make, and consumers didn't get worked up over a dead mouse in the mix. It was easy money.

At times the prison fare included McDonald's McRib sandwiches, procured through the finagling of Mr. Powers, the food manager.* During inmate strikes, Lieutenant Dodd remembers dietary repercussions for prisoners. Without inmate help in the kitchen, the kitchen staff prepared bologna sandwiches and supplied the prisoners, in their cells, with two sandwiches, an apple and usually a cookie.*

13

Prison is for Dings

In America we like to send the mentally ill to prison, and I found many folks in prison with lots (sometimes way too much) going on in their heads. We had different names for them, the most politically correct of which was mentally ill. The term I used was dings. As an inmate, the problem with dings was they didn't respect the rules of prison. They didn't care what club you belonged to, or how strong you were. If a ding got upset with you, they would strike, without thought of repercussions. Dings were mavericks and, as such, best left alone. In prison dings offered entertainment and amusement, but also made the whole experience more dangerous. A ding might not be afraid of you just because you were part of the Bike Shop, and this made the prison balance of power uncertain. I tried to stay under the radar of dings. The last thing I wanted was for a ding to get a message from someone, imagined or real, that I should die, and he was the chosen assassin.

Lieutenant Dodd recalls that there was no maximum-security state mental health facility, so those folks ended up at Walla Walla, often in segregation. The first day he went to the segregation unit, Dodd noted three big bottles of medication (Haladol, Stelazine, and Thorzine) at the disposal of officers. These were all anti-psychotic drugs, some more powerful than others, and if the staff ever ran out, they just asked the medical unit for more. There was also a very long daily pill line at the hospital. From Dodd's perspective, there didn't appear to be control or accounting of the quantity of drugs being dispensed.*

Four wing was also known as the ding wing, because most of those who stayed there long-term were dings. Once a new inmate was sick of four wing's one-man cells, he could go to the lieutenant and ask to get out of four wing. The lieutenant would ask if the inmate had a new place to go, and if not, the housing lieutenant would call in the control room clerk and ask about cells for sale or rent. Now if the housing lieutenant just moved you anywhere, you would be in jeopardy from the current owners, sometimes serious jeopardy. Because of that threat, some inmates stayed in four wing longer than they wanted.

Four wing had four tiers with one-man cells, including concrete beds, sink and toilet combos, no electrical outlets and only one lamp that the inmate could control, built right into the wall.

In the ding wing anything could happen, and often did. The showers were in the front of the cell blocks A and B so at the prescribed time, inmates were let out of their cells for showers. Being the ding wing, personal hygiene was not a top priority for many, and so lots of them didn't bother showering. The stalls had dividers between the shower heads and so showering was fast, in and out--unless you had to wait for two guys ahead of you to quit having sex, right in front of everyone. The guards were supposed to make sure that didn't happen, but when dealing with dings it was safer for guards to just look the other way. Sex drive is a pretty strong drive and it was going to get satisfied one way or another, or else more serious injury might result.

There was a guy named Robbie who was a real tough guy. He lifted weights all the time and was in really good shape. He was so strong he tore an entire auto engine down using only channel lock pliers. His reason for using only the pliers: he didn't want to get any of the other tools dirty.

In the winter, Robbie walked around in the snow, bare-footed and wearing only jeans and a t-shirt. One day everything changed for Robbie. He showed up at breakfast wearing a mini dress and makeup with bright red lipstick. You probably can guess that Robbie was not quite right in the head—he was a true ding.

Vampire Jones was a little guy that talked to himself all the time. His nickname came from his licking the blood up off the sidewalks whenever it was spilt, which was about every day. He also liked to buy propane lighters from the inmate store.[31] Putting the lighter on the ground, he would light a book of matches and place them by the lighter. When he stomped on the lighter, it released all the propane at once and Vampire Jones would disappear in a ball of flames. It was a pretty dramatic show.

The staff dealt with this by cutting off his purchasing rights for lighters. Of course, that just meant that instead of paying 50 cents at the inmate store, he had to pay $1 from a fellow inmate for his lighters. Unfortunately, the only mental health support available was from the third floor, and a lot of strange things happened on the third floor. More on that to come.

This little ding named Dog Man had an invisible dog that went everywhere with him. He held the door for his dog and some of the guards brought treats for this dog. It was an interesting show in an otherwise predictable environment. The dog would roll over and do all manner of tricks. Finally, one day Dog Man got released. As he was leaving, the guard said, Hey, you better wait for your dog. Dog Man replied, I'm going home, and my mom doesn't care for dogs so he's yours now. My thinking was that he acted crazy, and convincingly so, that no one messed with him in prison.

Out in the industrial complex were the laundry, license plate factory, furniture factory, auto mechanics and office machine repair shop, as well as engineering, which was responsible for maintenance. In the auto mechanics/office machine repair office was a ding named Jewette. He was a strange little guy, which was very typical of dings. A coffee cup clipped to his belt earned him a place into the coffee cup carrying ding group. He even carried around some keys, which he found, and which didn't fit any locks, but carrying keys was not uncommon for dings; carrying keys gives a man a sense of power.

One day he was hanging around and I asked him why he was in the joint, even though it was generally considered bad manners to ask. Then again, my status as a Bike Shop member gave me more license to ask such questions.

---

31 Yes—propane lighters were being sold to inmates, though no staff member would admit that they gave the OK for these sales.

To my question, Jewette replied that he had bothered some women. Of course, I had to know how he had bothered them, so I asked him. He said, I would go to the park and get in a tree and when one would walk under the tree, I would jump out of the tree onto them and do the nasty. In prison we often referred to rapos as tree jumpers but I had never met a rapist who actually used that tactic. I asked him how he decided which ones to bother and he replied that he preferred the grannies. I asked him why that preference and he replied that his grandmother made his father get rid of his goat when she caught him doing the nasty with the goat.

Phillip was another interesting ding, who earned his way to prison by committing a bunch of burglaries, for which he was sent to Eastern State Hospital, a mental institution. While there he was caught in the shower with another man and, apparently, they took that stuff seriously at Eastern State, so he was sent to Walla Walla. He was around 22 years old and right away he had some trouble with guys wanting sexual relief. From my perspective, this problem commonly accompanied dings and Phillip seemed to kind of be into it anyway. Like most dings, Phillip was a loner and walked around a lot, talking to himself. At one point he got a boom box, of which he was quite proud. He took it to the big yard and laid down on the grass while listening to music. Another inmate sneaked up with a small radio tuned to the same station and put it down by Phillip's boom box, and then the other inmate took Phillip's boom box and snuck away with it.

This was great sport and everyone wanted to see how the ding would deal with it. Phillip woke up at 4:00 pm count and looked at the radio. He promptly announced that Dr. Spock had shrunk his radio. Then he launched into a screaming fit, ordering Scottie to beam him up and such. The guards took him back to his cell, but he didn't want to go because he needed to be beamed up in order for Dr. Spock to enlarge his radio. It took about five guards to wrestle him to the ground, meanwhile Phillip screaming for Scottie to beam him up.

Phillip was paroled and sent home, but he was back in less than six months for a parole violation. While on parole the bodies of three homeless men were found in Chelan County. All the bodies were beheaded.

When Phillip returned to prison, he got a job in the chapel, working with the Right Reverend Grant, a Protestant minister. Phillip had only six months to serve on his parole violation and so was a short-termer in prison. However, Phillip found higher meaning to life while working in the chapel, and became a changed man. The first thing Phillip did was confess his sins to the Right Reverend, assuming of course that the confession was received in confidence. His sins included killing and beheading the homeless folks in Chelan County and Phillip felt much better having confessed his sins. Unfortunately for Phillip, the Reverend didn't keep anything confidential and Phillip ended up serving two life sentences. Dings were never paroled when they were on a life sentence, so that wasn't a great result for Phillip. However, the brutality of the crimes earned Phillip some prison creds and his likelihood of being preyed upon was much decreased. Anyone who'd served time knew that dings were dangerous and no doubt Phillip was an example of that.

Big Yard baseball diamond.
Photo supplied by James Spalding, Director of Communications.

Jimmy Q was a skinny little guy, about 5'10" and 120 pounds, serving a life sentence for killing his girlfriend. I guess they had a fight and she somehow stopped breathing during the argument and so old Jimmy Q loaded her into the trunk and drove to the local hardware store to buy a shovel to bury the body. When he came out from the store, his car was missing. It was found several days later in a Sea Tac Airport parking lot, so it was off to Walla Walla for Jimmy Q. He had no friends and just wandered about the prison whenever he was released to general population. His habit of asking guys if he could pop their pimples tended to get him beat up on occasion.

Gordy and Miss Harold were a couple dings, living in the segregation unit as workers. They delivered meals and if there was an inmate in a cell causing trouble, a guard might say, Hey Gordy, the guy in seven wants to have sex with your mother again. If I was you, I would take the fire hose and hose him down. Generally, Gordy obliged, and to me it was all good sport, but for Gordy it meant that he was a dead man if he ever went to protective custody or back into the general population.

Gordy and Miss Harold had gotten married some time back, and before you knew it Miss Harold gave birth to a strapping young boy, often referred to as shit face the puppet by inmates. This child was kept wrapped in a towel and they appeared to take care of their baby as best they could.

One day a surprise shakedown of the segregation kitchen was ordered, and the baby was found alone in the kitchen. As near as could be determined, Officer Woody found the baby and flushed him down the toilet. Gordy, by this time, had been let out of his cell and he went berserk upon learning his son was murdered. He tore the segregation kitchen totally apart, then Miss Harold got wind of the news and joined in the destruction. They both ended up on the mental health floor of the hospital, where their care was supervised by Dr. Hunter, who was at least as crazy as any of his patients.

Crazy Charlie lived in the ding wing, in his one-man cell. He was serving two life sentences for killing some people in an apartment building that he owned in the Seattle area. Charlie used his background in chemistry to deal with some renters who were behind on rent and refused to move out. This apartment building had a big furnace in the basement with ducts going up to the individual apartments. Charlie went to the basement and opened the vent for the low-life, non-rent-paying couple's apartment and inserted a device that put poison gas into their ventilation system. Feeling euphoric and victorious, Charlie went to his apartment gleefully. To his surprise, the couple was up and about the next morning.

Now, most people would have second thoughts about killing someone in such a manner, but not Charlie. Charlie figured out his mistake (wrong vent tube) and the next night, he opened the correct vent and used the poisonous gas again, and this time it worked. With such obvious evidence of premeditation and intent, Charlie was convicted and sentenced to Walla Walla, which should have been the end of Charlie's criminal spree.

After Charlie was in the joint for a year, people in four wing started getting attacked on a regular basis by some guys running a bill collecting business. The Bike Shop's Secret Police got a tip that Charlie had lots and lots of cash in white money, not prison script, in his cell.

Prison governance decided that Charlie needed to start paying for some protection, both for his own good and to stabilize the institution's power structure. Charlie was told to pony up $500 or to check into protective custody. Charlie went to his cell and came back with $500, which was apparently no big sacrifice. Now Charlie couldn't order assaults without first getting approval for the attack and paying taxes on his income. Everyone was happy, for a time.

One day he let it be known that he wanted an old guy really beaten up. This old guy was of great value to the Bike Shop's Secret Police, as he had supplied a wealth of good information, and no one in the Bike Shop wanted to lose him. However, Charlie really wanted this guy hurt, because he offered $1000 for the attack and in the late 1970s in prison, that was a whole lot of money. Eventually the $1000 was paid, without taxes paid, and so Charlie instead of the old guy got beat up.

With Charlie the Ding bruised and beat up, the staff grew worried about him and they searched his one-man cell. All Charlie had for personal effects was a four-foot high stack of old newspapers, which the sergeant ordered thrown out. Charlie went crazy when he learned his newspapers were missing, and actually had to be restrained by guards. Eventually Charlie told the guards that he had some money hidden in the papers. Yeah, some money turned out to be over $10,000 in cash.

As far as his murder convictions went, Charlie had so much money *before going to prison* that he had hired the best attorneys. His sentence for the two murders resulted in him serving less than 10 years for the convictions.

The Good Right Reverend Nightlinger, as he called himself, was an inmate that spent hours in his cell writing up religious tracts to hand out at the chow hall. He stood outside as people entered the chow hall and handed out these tracts, all the while preaching about Jezebels and harlots, and such.

The Good Reverend was in prison for killing those whom the Lord required slain. He was a little man, maybe not even five feet, really thin, and in his late 60s or early 70s. He always wore a navy stocking cap and had this golf ball-sized knot on his forehead. He looked like he could have played a dwarf in *Snow White*.

Every Sunday in prison we got steak for dinner and that was a real treat. The reverend had the habit of giving a very long prayer before eating. One Sunday the reverend sat down and started his prayer. Meanwhile, an inmate tip-toed over and stole his steak. When the reverend finished, everyone was quiet and watching to see how he would react, expecting some good entertainment.

When the reverend noticed that his steak was gone, he jumped up and threw his tray across the room. He then vaulted atop a table and pulled out a Roman short sword, screaming about demons and filthy Jezebels. This brought the prison guards, who convinced him to lay down his weapon and go with them. He went to the third floor of the hospital and was put in the care of Dr. Hunter. This experience underscored to me the dangerous unpredictability of dings: even though the Good Reverend seemed mostly harmless, he obviously had triggers leading to unpredictable behaviors.

Gilbert Starks and Marvella lived in eight wing as a happy BPFU couple. They had a cell that looked like a house inside, with furniture and hand-carved tables. One night late you might hear someone getting slapped, then Marvella would holler, N....r, you hit me again and I'm gonna forget I'm a woman. In fact, Marvella was a prize fighter and no one to mess with. Then we'd hear Gilbert say, Bitch, you can't talk to your man that way. Then we'd hear furniture breaking while Marvella took Gilbert, a tall, thin guy, and used him as a battering ram. Next morning the formerly lovely house looked like a tornado had hit.

With all the mental health issues, of course drugs were a hot commodity. Lieutenant Dodd remembers that inmates that left the pill line at the hospital could swallow their medication, sell it, or have it strong-armed away. Inmates tried anything they could lay their hands on to extract a high. Lieutenant Dodd remembers working in the MSB and having an inmate keel over during dinner. The inmate then acquired a purple and green ring around the outside of his mouth, while foam began coming from inside his mouth. He was taken to the hospital where the preliminary (and correct) diagnosis was made as poisoning. Because dinner was still going on, Lieutenant Dodd announced to the assembled inmates what had happened and one inmate said that someone had brought in some powder, saying that it was speed. The poisoned inmate spread it on his meal and ate it. Turned out the speed was really some kind of rodent poison. After this exchange three additional prisoners asked to be taken to the infirmary. All four of the lucky prisoners survived.* When Dodd arrived in 1970, the big trend in sniffing was by using Vicks vapor inhalers.*

Later word got out that you could get a heroin high by sniffing shoe repair glue, and Barges glue was the top recommended brand. Suddenly the shoe repair guy was making a bundle selling his glue and it took no time for Jones from four wing to become addicted. He was a ding, living in four wing, with no support group, either in prison or in the free world, which was pretty typical for dings.

The way we saw it, glue sniffing kills off brain cells a little each time you use it, so you get a little dumber day by day. Jones didn't have many cells to spare and in any other country, Jones would have been in a mental hospital. He wasn't long into his glue sniffing before he forgot how to eat with silverware and, of course, lost control of his bodily functions. Now, broke from feeding his addiction and in worse health than ever, he believed the answer to his woes was to coat his privates in the glue and get high sniffing it that way. Being glue and sticky and all, this was not a great idea. It was his unlucky ticket to the third floor of the hospital and Dr. Hunter's "care." I'm not sure how Jones fared under Dr. Hunter's treatment.

I've talked about Dr. Hunter a few times . . . now the real skinny on the prison's mental health unit and its physician. Dr. William Hunter ran the third floor of the hospital, which was the prison's mental health program. This was the Neverland of the prison; regular prison staff would take people there and just leave them to the third-floor staff. Everyone— prisoners and staff alike—understood that the third floor was no place to be. Way too many deaths happened there, including people who hung themselves with their hands tied behind their backs.[32]

Prison staff received direct instruction from Rhay to leave this area to the mental health staff; everyone knew there was a whole lot of really bad stuff going on there. Dr. Hunter used a "goon squad" of "cured" patients to monitor, harass and terrify prisoners that were "in-treatment." The goon squad seemed to use some especially sadistic form of aversion therapy, where the first transgression resulted in some trivial consequence, and the consequence getting worse for each additional infraction. The ultimate punishment was strapping a prisoner to a cot wearing nothing but a diaper, while the goon squad doled out punishment through methods that often included hypodermic needles of medicine. One state review of Dr. Hunter's methods found it effective in changing behavior, but at the same time frighteningly similar to the tactics Mao used on US prisoners of war during the Korean conflict.[33] Finally, in 1975, it took a lawsuit to close down the third floor of the hospital.[34] I felt like Dr. Hunter was responsible, directly or indirectly, for a lot of deaths, and a basic survival

32 Murray at 102.
33 Murray at 105.
34 Murray at 106-8.

instinct told all the prisoners to stay away from his third-floor treatment ward.

Though things seemed pretty off-kilter to me, there weren't a lot of avenues for complaint. There was an office called Prison Legal Services, which mostly dealt with inmate divorces and property issues. However, the lawyers there could do civil rights actions or class actions, including lawsuits pushing for prison reforms, and eventually they started lawsuits aimed at improving prison life. One of these civil rights lawsuits, involving an inmate and former patient of Dr. Hunter's named Michael Brookshire, ultimately managed to close down Dr. Hunter's clinic.[35] Unfortunately this didn't happen until untold abuses and deaths occurred under the direction and leadership of Dr. Hunter.

---

35 Murray at 68.

14

Death in Prison

Stink Finger Bass was a quiet little ding who lived in four wing. He was a young black man in his early 20s and never bothered anyone. He got his name because he wore a jumpsuit that had a bass fisherman's patch on the shoulder, and he had a habit of sniffing one finger in particular through the cotton gloves he always wore.

In the late 1970s the Monroe Reformatory had a lot of trouble with their inmates, and many young prisoners had been sent to the Walla Walla. While going to the education department, I was walking behind two of these young transfers from Monroe. I was minding my own business, drinking my rum and Coke that I had picked up at the Coke Shack, which was run by a free world man. Incidentally, this free world man had been "overly friendly" with one of the prison girls and somehow a Polaroid had captured the encounter on film. It was assumed that his wife (and others) would frown upon the activity depicted in the photo, so the free world man was indebted to certain prisoners in authority. This man just couldn't take the pressure and he quit his job about six months later. Funds from the MSB Coke Shack were used to build a handball court and buy pool tables for the inmates.*

As I walked behind these two Monroe transfers, I overheard one of them say, "What we need to do is kill someone and get a reputation." This didn't concern me because I am in the Bike Shop and Bike Shop members never made the hit list of such punks, even though both of these guys were affiliated with their own gang, the Gay Liberation Army. Under the prison power structure, the Gay Liberation Army sounded official, but it didn't inspire actual fear or even respect within the general population.

One night in the movie hall these two decided to get that sought-after reputation. Stink Finger was sitting in the back of the theater with some other dings from four wing, all enjoying a night out on the town at the theater. It was alleged that one of the two Monroe punks took a Roman short sword (to call it a knife would not do justice to the weapon, because it had a longer blade than a knife) and stabbed Stink Finger in the chest, pinning him to his theater chair. Activity like this almost always caused a rush to the door as half the audience tried to rush out, all at the same time.

The theater officer turned on the lights and there were several of the working girls, half-naked, with their Johns, and then there was Stink Finger, pinned to his seat, dead as a door nail.

Now the theater was full of rats, and in no time the killers were rounded up. Prosecuting attorney Arthur E. Eggers again assured the prison staff that his team, asking for the death penalty, would get a conviction. We had all heard this before.

The trial was a great one, as one of the killers testified that he was not in the theater that night, but instead at eight wing, receiving anal sex with a prisoner. Any old granny on the jury knew that had to be true, because no one would make up a story like that, even to protect himself from a murder charge. Both accused were found not guilty.

Connie's message was still alive and well to the residents of Walla Walla: the prisoners will handle their own problems, and no burden will be placed on the residents of Walla Walla to deal with their issues. Several years later the Walla Walla Union Bulletin had an article on things found plugging up the sewer system and the article showed a picture of the items found. Among the things found was the prisoner ID card of Stink Finger Bass.

15

Walla Walla's Medical Treatment

Treatment for more basic medical issues besides mental health was also lacking at the prison. As a prisoner, I learned this lesson well when a friend of mine, Brother Redwine, was murdered. He was a kindhearted black man, member of the BPFU, and in his late 20s or early 30s. I remember him as smart, gentle and easy to get along with. I knew him from the prison's college program, where Brother Redwine also was working on his four-year degree. His nickname of Professor Wine came from the long-winded questions he liked to ask in class. I knew him from several of my classes, and sometimes his questions did not have much to do with the subject at hand. I liked this because it used up classroom time and nothing he asked about would ever be on the test, so it gave us a break from notetaking.

One day, Brother Redwine got into an argument with another inmate and was stabbed in the stomach. He was rushed to the prison hospital, where he received horrible medical care. At first a chest x-ray and blood study were ordered, but then that was cancelled, and the cut was just sewn back together. Though he was ordered back to his cell by the doctor, custody refused to move him and left him in the hospital.

Later that night Brother Redwine had blood all over him, soaking through his pajamas and sheets. An x-ray technician took the initiative and, without doctor's orders, x-rayed Brother Redwine's chest, finding the small bowel dilated. The physician yelled at the x-ray technician for taking the x-ray and did nothing to deal with the bleeding. Instead, I later found out, Brother Redwine lay in bed the next day, hugging his abdomen, until he was found dead toward evening. The cause of death was from internal hemorrhaging.[36] His murderers (both the inmate that knifed him and the physician that ignored him) were never punished, though his death was later used in a civil rights lawsuit to demonstrate the brutality of the prison.[37]

Lieutenant Dodd remembers working as shift lieutenant and entering the area where the license plates came in on a conveyer belt after being painted. He found an inmate lying on the floor, so badly injured that the only way you could tell he was alive were the bubbles coming out of his lips as he wheezed. Dodd immediately called for a downtown ambulance, and also dispatched two officers to escort the ambulance through the gate. The ambulance came and the inmate was taken directly to the downtown hospital, where the staff agreed with his decision to send the inmate directly to the downtown hospital. However, Dodd later caught hell from his supervisor for making that call, as the supervisor didn't think the prisoner's injury justified sending him to an outside hospital.*

Another time Dodd responded to a call for officers to the cell blocks, where he found medical staff checking on an inmate, lying on the floor. The inmate had an inch of white syrup all along his body that looked like his bodily fluids leaking out. Dodd listened as the medical staff told the other officers that the inmate had just had a seizure and that they should just put him back in his bunk. Dodd over-rode that assessment and told the officers to load him on a gurney and take him to the hospital. Weeks later the patient's cellmate thanked Dodd, telling him that if he hadn't been sent to medical his cellmate would have died.*

In spite of its shortcomings and shortcuts, Dodd maintains great admiration for the medical staff, who worked under very stressful conditions.* Working in the hospital was one job that Dodd admits he would never want. Medical staff were assaulted, held hostage, threatened and verbally abused; it took a very special person to work in prison medical.* In some ways the prison hospital was a draw to local doctors, because they could see medical cases that they didn't usually find in Walla Walla.* One example was in the early days of AIDS cases.

---

36 Murray at 247-49.
37 Hoptowit v. Ray 682 F.2d 1237 (9th Cir., 1985).

Because Walla Walla was a maximum-security facility, they could house inmates with diseases requiring isolation. One such prisoner was a violent man with AIDS, initially housed in the Intensive Management Unit, but later moved to the hospital as his health deteriorated. For whatever reason, the inmate blamed the treating doctor for giving him AIDS and told the staff that he would bite that doctor the next time he tried to treat him. Dodd and two corrections officers accompanied the doctor on his next examination of the inmate. Dodd and the officers entered the examination room first and the inmate said, "I do not want any trouble with you." Dodd replied that he wouldn't have trouble, as long as he didn't cause the doctor any trouble. The inmate said, "OK,' and the doctor entered and examined the inmate and then left, after which Dodd and the corrections officers followed. Eventually the inmate committed suicide, leaving his blood everywhere.

In time, Walla Walla had an inmate with AIDS in general population. One morning about 9:00 am Dodd got a call that the inmate had cut himself several times and died, bleeding out in his cell. According to prison procedures when a prisoner is already dead, his body was left alone for the county coroner to make the first examination. After the coroner arrived and released the body, the hospital administrator warned every one of his AIDS condition. Dodd returned to his office and soon a phone call came in from his unit officer, stating that the hospital administrator told him (the unit officer) to go clean up the blood. Dodd responded that the officer should not do so: they lacked training to clean up hazardous waste. As a prisoner, I always thought it was strange the way that AIDS prisoners kept knifing themselves; it happened more than once that I can recall.

The hospital administrator stormed into Dodd's office protesting, followed by a call from the prison Superintendent. Dodd presented his (correct) appraisal that whomever cleaned up the blood needed training in hazardous disposal, whether that be an inmate crew or officers. A half an hour later a hospital crew arrived and cleaned up the mess, with the hospital administrator doing a lot of the work. Quickly thereafter a crew of inmates were trained to clean up hazardous messes at the rate of $1 per cleanup.*

Another time Lieutenant Dodd arrived at work to learn that a maximum-security inmate was hit in the head with free weights. Because the back of his skull was caved in, he was flown to Seattle for medical care. Dodd ordered the free weights moved from the area, though the recreation director took issue with that decision. The Superintendent again called Dodd in to her office and Dodd explained his position: the free weights were a danger to all inmates, and therefore many inmates were likely happy to have them gone, given the assault.*

During the early 1970s there were a lot of murders, mostly accompanied with rumors regarding the assailant, but with a dead victim, there was seldom credible testimony. One shift Lieutenant Dodd heard a passing prisoner tell him to check out the recreation bathrooms. When Dodd pushed the door open, it stopped halfway, resting against the long legs of a 6'6" inmate. The inmate had a large puncture wound to his neck, and all his blood had obviously pumped out onto the restroom floor. By the time Dodd got there, it looked like a big pile of gelatin, about four inches thick, sliding down his body and onto the ground two feet around. When the coroner showed up and moved the body, he found a pair of barber's scissors underneath. The coroner ruled the death a suicide. Another murder occurred when an inmate, seated and playing his guitar, was stuck with an icepick-type shank. The shank went up under his breastbone and killed him instantly. When Dodd arrived, the inmate was dead, though still sitting up. In November 1973, Dodd was in the control room when an inmate came walking up the breezeway, holding his right side. Dodd sent him to the hospital and then twenty minutes later listened as the inmate started screaming in the hospital. The screaming continued for some time, then quit abruptly when the inmate died. The cause of death was a stick to either the kidney or liver.*

16

The Bike Shop

To me, all of this mayhem said that something was wrong with the power structure of the prison, and something needed to change. This change came when the Bike Shop took control of the prison, bringing some modicum of peace. In the mid-1970s, the Bike Shop's president was named Mike Abrams, and his administration marked transition of the shop into a powerful force in the prison. Mike started teaching prisoners how to repair motorcycles. In the process, he began a public relationship committee to contact people and groups on the outside, seeking their sponsorship and help. In time, I headed the public relations committee and was given responsibility of picking four members to help me in this work. Those foolish enough to admit they could type were chosen.

We wrote individual, unique letters to every motorcycle shop in Washington and Oregon, telling them of our work in teaching prisoners motorcycle repair skills, and soliciting donations to further our work. We also wrote to politicians at state and federal levels, and within six months, donations were pouring in from congressional members, judges, attorneys general, and sheriff's departments, as well as bike shops. We sold our program as a success by pointing to our club's high level of participation, as well as its availing of a marketable vocational skill, all being done without cost to the government. The sky-high attendance rate at club meetings was more likely due to the heavy hand of the club president, not necessarily interest or commitment on the part of the prisoner. Nonetheless, our program was seen as a model program for other prisons and was featured on national and local news.

The Bike Shop became so powerful, and the prison practices were such, that our clubhouse could not be searched by even prison officials without prior authorization from the club leadership. Lieutenant Dodd recalls that because of inadequate staffing, the prison simply didn't have the manpower to conduct clubhouse or cell searches.* If a guard was pursuing an inmate for an infraction and a clubhouse door stopped him, then that was that; there was no going beyond the locked door without the clubhouse's permission.[38] Bike Shop members were generally not searched without permission from the warden. Also, Bike Shop endorsement became a necessary feature of any prison guard application for promotion. When Warden Rhay was replaced, Bike Shop members sat on the panel that chose the new warden.

At some point, guards had all but given up on controlling prisoners, or enforcing rules. In 1974, when Jim Harvey came to Walla Walla as assistant superintendent, he estimated that 95% of corrections officers had given up doing their jobs. One prisoner said that, only when the prison gangs failed to control the violence, were guards asked to do their jobs. Guards mostly stayed out of the way of the prisoners.[39] [40]

In April 1975 the RGC was replaced by the Resident Council. This change, contrary to expectations, resulted in an even more weakened administration, and power, like nature, abhors a vacuum. In the absence of power-wielding by an administration-sanctioned council, gangs like the Bike Shop, Lifers and BPFU, flourished.[41]

This power structure was neither good nor bad really, but just inevitable given the circumstances. After all, someone had to be in charge if the administration wasn't. The bikers were unique in discipline and unity, which allowed them to channel their power in such a way that they could accomplish whatever they felt was important. One guard later

---

38 Murray at 111.
39 Murray at 109.
40 This is a sweeping statement that certainly didn't apply to all corrections officers. Among the 5% were corrections officer that enjoyed abusing prisoners. Murray at 112.
41 Murray at 114.

said, "During particularly dangerous times [in the prison], bikers would stand shoulder to shoulder with correctional officers." When coming off lockdown, a notoriously volatile time, everywhere you saw a corrections officer, you saw a biker standing next to him.[42]

42 Murray at 119.

17

Prisoner Secret Police

After having a very successful fundraising response from the public relations campaign I oversaw, Bike Shop president Mike Abrahams decided that I had further leadership potential in organizing club projects. Our numbers had dwindled as the club purged heavy drug users from membership and an emphasis was placed on members having a working knowledge of motorcycles, or at least vehicles. Contrary to popular opinion, in my experience bikers don't use a lot of drugs, mostly because hard drug use makes you unreliable. Mike thought we could build a Secret Police, modeled after the Geheime Staatspolizei during World War II. The goal was to keep up with everything happening within the walls of the prison. In order to do that, the shop enlisted the help of ousted members whose only real loyalty was to an income that could purchase additional drugs. These ousted members provided information in exchange for money, and as an added bonus, the Bike Shop kept tabs on them. At the same time, Mike appointed me Vice President of External Affairs.

This operation was so secret that only Mike, our club president, I and one other member knew of its existence. The BPFU agreed to support this effort, because it would curtail some of the prison violence. Under the agreement, a small tax on drug dealers would fund our informant ring. I wanted to know everything that was going on. If some ding was planning a murder, we wanted to know about it in time to stop it. Senseless violence was really bad for everyday business.

Soon this operation started spying on staff members, to see if some dirt emerged that might prove profitable. It was amazing how easily this dirt surfaced. The head engineer, Walt Burfitt, was discovered to be having an affair with the inmate store lady, even though his wife was dying from cancer. Once this was documented with a Polaroid (the cameraman was hiding in the chicken ranch), Mr. Burfitt was no longer able to trash the Bike Shop as he had in the past. He even became a keen supporter of our efforts. Once word was out that our organization was interested in private staff conduct, a lot of interesting information poured in.

Also, bikers seemed able to get their hands on most anything. One time prison Sgt Helgeson lost his hat and hat badge and was worried about the consequences if supervisors found out. Early 1970s, Dodd recalls a humorous incident, Lt Colombo came to him reporting that Sgt Helgeson, while working in the kitchen dining hall, had his hat and badge stolen, and Lt Colombo wanted it back NOW. At the time, the Bike Shop ran everything in the prison, so I took my key to the Bike Shop, which I found in my travels, for at that time the officers did not have a key available to enter the Bike Shop. Officers had to go knock on the door to get permission to enter. I entered using my key and catching everyone off guard. Tommy Music I recognized at once, and he was shocked, as were other members, that I had gotten in unannounced. I proceeded to tell them the sad tale of Sgt Helgeson losing his hat and badge, which they all found humorous. I told them it won't be so funny if I didn't get the hat and badge back NOW. I told them it won't be so funny when I have this place torn apart. Tommy said, "Give me a few minutes, and we will see what we can find out."

On arriving back to the control room, Lt Colombo immediately wanted to know when the hat and badge would be recovered. I told him we expected to hear something soon.

Tommy showed up with the hat and badge and asked if the Shop would be torn apart now, and I assured him it would not be.

Sgt Helgeson immediately announced that it was not his, though it appeared to be the correct size, and no one else had announced losing their hat and badge. I told the sergeant that I would just keep them then. The sergeant then had a change of heart and said he would keep it, not wanting to have to face his superiors and explain how such a loss had occurred.*

This whole operation was set up so it appeared that Lifers like Warren Halverson were running the system. I don't think anyone ever guessed that actually it was being run by only three members of the Bike Shop. You can accomplish a lot when power perceived is power achieved. As the informants moved through the prison, the Bike Shop gained access to information on all prisoners, no matter where they were housed. Our informants learned that good information got good pay, and the information just poured in.

In the mid-1970s Associate Superintendent Harvey put Sergeant Dodd (eventually Lieutenant Dodd) in charge of a squad that did shakedowns. His goon squad was almost immediately renamed the "Dodd Squad." I had a lot of respect for him in that he never asked his men to do something he wouldn't do himself; he was always the first one into a cell. Also, he made sure the men working with him were fair in their treatment of inmates. You knew when Dodd pulled you over, you didn't have to worry about something being planted on you; you were either clean or dirty, with no help from Dodd.

Lieutenant Dodd was told to pick three officers for his squad, and then Associate Warden Harvey chose the fourth.* In December 1975, Dodd was told that a .38 caliber was found in the Lifers clubhouse, and so his squad was asked to shakedown their clubhouse, looking for more weapons. After two hours of searching, the squad noticed some false walls. They took down the wall and found an old .45-automatic pistol, fully loaded. The clip was taped on with duct tape since the clip latch was broken. In between the walls, along with the pistol, were one set of binoculars, one 5-watt handheld radio, two 2-watt handheld radios, 5 rounds of .45 caliber ammunition, 19 rounds of .38 caliber ammunition, 3 knives and over 200 feet of strong, nylon rope, a set of lock picks, a set of car keys, keys for the Nine Tower Gate, miscellaneous pills and about $3 in loose change.*

One thing I didn't realize at the time was how under-supplied the guards were. Here these inmates had radios, even though the guards hadn't yet been supplied with them. Two weeks later Dodd asked prison administration if they could use the radios; these were the first radios their unit had, and they could use them on their patrols. Dodd's lieutenant authorized him to go buy four more radios, though accounting denied the request because the state had a contract with another radio manufacturer. Finally, in early 1976, the guards got a base station and eight hand-held radios.* Older staff seemed to resist the move toward radios and eventually Dodd learned why: many had hearing loss from a lifetime of shooting guns without ear protection, and they couldn't hear through the radios without handheld microphones.*

Other firearms were recovered from throughout the prison. Dodd recalls recovering a .22 pistol in eight wing (inside a radio), as well as a .38 pistol from St. Peter in 1978.*

18

The Water Tower

In the middle of People's Park was a 150-foot high water tower that supplied water to the prison. Before eight wing and seven wing were built, the tower sat outside the walls. When the prison was expanded it put the tower inside the walls. Not a good plan. The water tower was a magnet for trouble and should never have been put inside the prison yard. Once a young inmate, trying to evade other inmates who were pressuring him, climbed the water tower. When one of the pressuring inmates started climbing up after him, the young inmate jumped, hitting a crosspiece on the way down and slamming to the ground. His fall compacted the cold winter ground about six inches; the inmate did not survive.*

One hot day in summer, a French Canadian (known as Frency, whose real name was Thomas Wagner) decided to occupy the water tower, so he climbed up the support cables to the ladder and then to the top of the tower and refused to come down. After a couple of days, news of this spread and there were airplanes flying by, taking photos. One became known as 8 o'clock Charlie for he flew by each night at 8 o'clock. Next Frency sent a list of grievances, which were presented to the staff. If his demands were met, then Frency and the others would come down from the tower.

The answer from the staff was "no." Now the hatch on the water tower was thrown open and the guys were all swimming in the tank. This contaminated the water, and an order came down from Olympia to meet some of the demands. Frency later got some black paint and painted his initials (FTW) on the water tower. The press wondered what it stood for and finally decided it must mean "F___ the World." That amused me; the press was quick to assume an obscenity, when what he wrote was really just ordinary juvenile graffiti.

Showing the top of Frency Wagner's water tower.
Photo supplied by James Spalding, Director of Corrections.

Bottom section of Frency Wagner's water tower in People's Park. Photo supplied
by James Spalding, Director of Corrections.

This entire incident took about two weeks, and the tower was taken over several more times, in spite of the administration's best efforts to prevent it; later they had greased the support cables and moved the ladder higher.

Sergeant Dodd remembers a prisoner who, with two of his buddies, climbed the water tower and refused to come down. Eventually they brought in the prisoner's mother, who was supposed to talk her son down. Instead, after saying "Hi" to one another, the mother said, "Son, you stay up there as long as you want. We are behind you all the way." Warden Rhay then ordered Dodd to get the woman out of there, though she managed to continue shouting encouragement to her wayward son.*

Penitentiary viewed from the outside 1960s. Frency Tower in upper right.

19

The Great Escape Attempt

One winter evening, in about November, there was a lot of fog in Walla Walla County, especially near the prison. During such times, inmates have lots of freedom within the walls, staying out until 8:45 pm without any special pass. My cell partners were James Neil Fogle[43] and David Riel, two weeks prior they announced to me that we should blow out of this dump. I took them seriously, because they had a lot of experience in this sort of thing.

The plan was to ease up on Six Tower Gate, directly north of the chow hall. We picked a Friday night and applied a little pressure to the entertainment committee to show a strong R- or X-rated movie that night. A skin flick would keep the riff raff out of our way. Because Jim had a really good speed[44] connection, he could easily make something like that happen. Six Tower Gate served as the entrance to the industrial area, allowing vehicles into the prison through its big, roll-up door.

All three of us worked out in the industrial area so, as we were leaving the industrial area one day, the Six Tower Gate guard, good old Woody, opened the roll-up gate for a cart of materials we brought into the prison yard. Jim commented to Woody that the door looked like it was struggling to go up, and maybe the electrician should look it. The chief engineer had been caught with his pants down on Polaroid film (remember Walt Burfitt?) and he didn't want anyone to find out about it. Using the picture as blackmail, I became the electrician for the prison.

---

43 James Fogle's story was made into a movie in the 1980s based on his book called *Drug Store Cowboy*.
44 Methamphetamine. Back then we called it speed.

I told Woody that I would come by with a guy from the metal shop and we would take a look at it. My friend Little Dave from the metal shop met me at the front of Six Tower Gate and I brought some donuts for Woody. For a guard, Woody was alright.

Metal Shop. Photo supplied by James Spalding, Director of Corrections.

The donuts worked magic in occupying Woody and as Woody was eating the donuts, Little Dave "fixed" the gate. The gate's problem, from our perspective, was that it had a lock so it couldn't be raised unless the lock was released. First thing Little Dave removed the lock, and we were ready for launch.

On this first good foggy Friday night (we got weather reports on the inside), the staff was working to have the water tower moved outside the prison yard, so there was a chain link fence surrounding People's Park. This left the area desolate, which served our purposes nicely. We also had a couple of lookouts posted in the kitchen to warn us if a guard was coming toward us. These lookouts were carefully selected: St. Peter and Squid Thomas, two trustworthy guys.

A shot of People's Park.
Photo supplied by James Spalding, Director of Corrections.

We thought we had it all figured out, using the fog as cover, but the fog brought cold and damp. We were walking from the kitchen to the wall by Six Tower Guard and then back, trying to look like we were just getting some exercise when actually we were trying not to freeze. Little Dave had a six-ton jack with an adapter, which fit under the frame of the rollup door. This jack could push the door up and allow our escape.

Dave Riel, James Fogle, Little Dave and I walked up to the wall by Six Tower seven or eight times. The last time Little Dave peeled off from us and covered himself with a blanket, while lying on the ground next to the roll-up gate. Freedom was only seconds away, it seemed.

Then we noticed our two kitchen lookouts Squid Thomas and St. Peter gone from their post, which we scarcely believed. These were top-notch, trustworthy escape artists, shirking their duties! Then we saw Sergeant Thompson, aka Hog Jowls Thompson, walking toward us. He saw us walking our way back toward the kitchen while Little Dave was lying on the ground, jacking up the gate. We knew the jig was up. Hog Jowls nabbed Little Dave and hauled him off to segregation, much to our dismay. We knew Hog Jowls had made us as well, and so, we walked toward our cell, in six wing down by the theater, by way of the control room. We stopped at the control room on our way back, talking to Sergeant Dodd for a minute and asking him what time it was.

Front entrance into the Control Room.
Photo supplied by James Spalding, Director of Corrections.

Little Dave was charged with attempted escape, while I, David Riel, and James Fogle were called to testify against him. The three of us stuck to our story, which was that we hadn't seen Little Dave while we were walking about and, in fact, when Little Dave was captured, James Fogle testified that the three of us were at the Control Room, talking to Captain Cataract. Captain Spalding was in charge of the court and demanded to know who Captain Cataract was. Fogle said, "Geezes Pard," then to Captain Spalding, "You know—the sergeant with the funny eye." [45] We then went on the list of undesirables for five or six years. Spalding would later become prison warden, then Director of Corrections for Washington and Idaho.

---

45 In the joint nicknames flourished. As far as nicknames go, Captain Cataract wasn't bad compared to Officer Marigold, for instance.

20

Close Call for Sergeant Dodd

Mike Ede was a curious little guy, who always wore a little hat like Bing Crosby or Dick Van Dyke. The story went that he was a transfer from San Quentin in a prisoner exchange. He was a Lifer and was invited to join the bike shop. At first, he was a right-on guy, but then he started getting paranoid. Let me explain.

We had two outlaw chapters within the bike shop, and this made Mike a little uneasy, because though he was a member of the bike shop, he didn't belong to either chapter. The fact that only half of the shop belonged to either of the two chapters didn't make Mike feel any better about it. So, Mike started going around feeling out members on starting a third chapter (an Aryan Brotherhood chapter) inside the shop. If an Aryan brother was assaulted by one of the members from another shop chapter, then the Aryan brothers would step in to protect the Aryan member. The plan made Mike feel at ease, even though it didn't make any sense. The reality was that shop members never assaulted fellow members, unless the leadership sanctioned it when the member needed to be taught a lesson, and that was really rare.

Mike went about recruiting for his Aryan chapter, but almost immediately everyone approached came to me and shared what Mike was doing. The president was not keen on Mike's idea, and neither was I. So, the prison's own little Bing Crosby got a good talking-to from shop leadership, and he left the bike shop. Because Mike was keen on drugs, it was likely best that he left the shop. Drugs made for more complicated relationships with members.

This left Mike an ex-bike shop member, though his former membership earned him some extra respect in the prison population. Once he was out of the shop, rumors began circulating that he was in protective custody while in San Quentin. When I heard this, my first thought was that they had some really tough rats in San Quentin if that rumor was true, but I didn't give it much more thought.

Soon I got a report from Squid Thomas and Warren Halverson that Mike was using a lot of speed (meth nowadays), and that Mike's paranoia was in high gear. Apparently, Mike was saying that, because so many people thought he was a rat, he was going to have to kill a few people, just to show everyone that he was a stand-up guy. Before anything happened, Mike was told that if he began just killing people, the backlash would be swift and severe (i.e., death).

Mike then changed his tune, slightly: he decided he would just kill some guards instead. I didn't think he was serious. I thought he was just trying to save face after being told that he wouldn't be allowed to go on a killing spree among the prisoners. I was wrong.

One day a non-bike shop member ran to the shop to report that Mike was crazy high, and that guards were taking him to the control room. Earlier in the day Mike had been flashing a weapon and talking about killing some guards. Since the source of the information was very reliable, a prospect was sent to spy on the control room. Soon we got a report that Sergeant Dodd and Lieutenant Sanders were stabbed. As it turned out, Lieutenant Hanson was stabbed also. In any case, Dodd remembers it like this:

One afternoon Sergeant Dodd reported to his shift as the control room desk sergeant when two guards came out of eight wing looking upset. One told Dodd that a prisoner named Mike Ede was high on drugs. Dodd asked if they'd informed the shift lieutenant and they said they had, but that since the shift was almost over, the shift lieutenant told them to leave it to the next shift to deal with. Sergeant Dodd took the news to his lieutenant, who told him to get Mike Ede sent up to the control room.

Ten minutes later Mike came walking up the breezeway and was cleared into the waiting room. The shift sergeant, looking at Mike through the window, could tell he was loaded. This shift sergeant, not one to stare danger in the face, said, I don't want any part of that, and left. Meanwhile, Mike was shook down before going into the office with two lieutenants. Mike entered the room and Dodd went in behind him, blocking the door should Mike decide to bolt through it.

Dodd intentionally stood close to Mike, knowing that he had been shook down already and was therefore unarmed. Also, Dodd knew it would be hard for Mike to land a hard punch when Dodd was so close to him.

Suddenly, Mike reached into his pants retrieving a knife, then dropped to a crouch. Immediately Mike swiveled around and stabbed upward with his knife in his left hand. Dodd deflected the knife and the knife stuck Dodd in the right shoulder paralyzing the arm and cutting an artery. The knife stick folded Dodd in half.

Several corrections officers swarmed to the room. As Dodd swirled around to grab Mike, his arm would not function. Officer Page grabbed and dragged Dodd out of the room and harm's way. Mike also slashed Lt Sanders and stabbed Lt Hanson twice in the leg. After Mike was cuffed, Dodd, stunned and uncertain how badly he was injured, made his way to the hospital, spraying blood as he went. At some point a corrections officer joined Dodd on his walk and supported him as he made his way to the hospital. When the 30 or so inmates waiting at the hospital in the pill line took a look at Dodd, bloody, spraying blood and holding his arm, they scattered. John Croll, ripped Dodd's shirt off and tied his arm off. Dodd reported, "It really hurts like hell." Office Sam Weber drove Dodd to Walla Walla Hospital.

Next both lieutenants in the office with Mike and Dodd also came walking in. All three were quickly bandaged and driven to the county hospital. The lieutenant that was cut to his breastbone was admitted to the hospital, while the other lieutenant and Dodd returned to the prison at 4:30 pm with Lt Hanson. Though his right arm still wasn't functioning (he couldn't lift it because of the severed nerves), Dodd put on a clean shirt and borrowed a jacket from Officer Snell.* It was way too small, but Dodd was able to use it as a sling, which no one noticed was a Walla Walla Sheriff Department jacket. While Dodd helped with chow line for dinner, one of the eight wing prisoners came by, looked at Dodd, and said, You're supposed to be dead. Dodd told him to shut up and eat.

After work, Dodd went with work friends to a bar and doesn't remember getting home. He was awakened at noon the next day by his wife. He got up and then went to work. Later that day his parents called and spoke with his wife after reading in the paper about the stabbing. Dodd had a constant reminder of the assault over the next five years: his shoulder tingled as the cut nerves healed.*

After this knifing, Bike Shop members were dispatched to walk with some officers. We needed to make sure this was an isolated event. We feared some dings might do a copycat killing in the control room, and that could be really bad for business.

On the left: Parley Edwards, center seated: My Uncle Cecil Hults called "Uncle Cees" by the Bike Shop. Photo taken by Ethan Hoffman.

21

Escape by Corvair

The prison's automobile club (WSPAA) had just restored a Corvair for a customer and parked it outside their clubhouse for a wash. Their clubhouse was next to a chain link gate, just 20 feet away from a big, iron gate heading out of the prison, supposedly for fire truck access only. Straight in front of the WSPAA clubhouse was a third truck gate, though this one had a rollup door. With all those gates there, I guess it made at least one prisoner think it was a good escape venue. Apparently, this area was staked out, and the practices of the WSPAA had been scrutinized. At least one escape-planning prisoner observed that keys were always left inside cars and trucks, since the risk of theft for an already-incarcerated vehicle seemed quite low.

Back then everyone (I thought) was aware that, according to Ralph Nadar, a Corvair was unsafe at any speed, especially if it was going to be abused while escaping from a penitentiary. Apparently, an inmate named Stinky Pants Frankie hadn't registered this tidbit of consumer warning, or maybe he just didn't care. However, a rear engine placement would protect the engine from damage. He had a choice of seven cars. Six with radiators up front and the Corvair with no radiator, so he was smarter than given credit for. And, before I go further recounting this incident, I need to mention that, to the WSPAA's credit, Stinky Pants Frankie was not a club member.

I think Frankie latched on to his plan of escape by television. Frankie had watched the General Lee on *Dukes of Hazard* crash through gates like they were made of paper, and thus Frankie's escape plan was hatched. Frankie showed how you can be crazy, but still crafty, especially when you zero in on an idea and exclude all distracting information. All the time people say that someone must not have been crazy, because how else could he have plotted such a scheme. Well, I know that you can be good and crazy and still plot out all manner of schemes, if you stay focused. Just because Stinky Frankie never changed his soiled underwear or combed his long, hippie hair, didn't mean he couldn't zero in on a plan.

Bo and Luke Duke had shown Frankie how to escape, and how to race off and meet all manner of cool hippie chicks, so Frankie was sold on the idea. His plan was to steal a WSPAA car, fire it up, and drive it through the gates to freedom, then meet up with a Charles Manson gal and live together in paradise.

But the Corvair (2300 pounds) was no Dodge Charger (4000 pounds) and the prison gates hadn't been engineered to part like cardboard, as Frankie learned. The pressed-box frame of the Corvair, which made the car so dangerous from the outset, was a large part of the problem.

Not comprehending this risk, Frankie doggedly pursued his plan and bought access to the car by paying a joint of weed to one of the car club guys. Frankie claimed he just wanted to sit in the car, while listening to the radio. In hindsight, it probably was a low-risk deal for the car club guy, since it wasn't like Frankie could just drive off with the car, and a joint to a druggie on the inside was a very tempting payoff. Besides, renting cars was a fairly common practice; cars were rented to couples wanting to have sex in the back seat.

Frankie's plan developed nicely, as he envisioned listening to the radio, with the engine purring so the battery wouldn't lose its charge, while listening to The Mamas and Papas on the radio. Frankie saw a path to the outside world and he even tasted freedom, if only for a moment. With the tires squealing and the smell of burnt rubber, the plan unfolded as the Corvair burst the chain link gate open, like the General Lee had so many times on television.

Gas pedal to the floor and visions of a Manson girl with her arms wide open for her hero, Frankie's hopes were stone-walled with a huge, metal-meets-metal bang. The 2300-pound Corvair did not make it through the steel firetruck gate, even with the engine winding at 5000 to 6000 rpm.

With Frankie slumped over the steering wheel, guards sprang up along the prison wall catwalks, all with guns drawn. Meanwhile inmates, hearing and seeing only part of the action, streamed in for a better look.

Tower that shot Frankie.

Lieutenant Dodd remembered that day. He heard three rapid shots and then ran towards Three Tower, finding a Corvair that had buckled the big, steel gate, but not gone through. He also saw three bullet holes (courtesy of the Three Tower guard) in the shape of a triangle about nine inches high on the driver's side of the Corvair. The car engine was still running and, as Dodd opened the driver's side door, Frankie fell out, asking, "What the hell is he shooting?" Guards had recently changed to using the M-1 universal carbine, which was apparently a surprise to Frankie. Frankie had been hit twice: one shell broke his left hip and another shell hit his right leg.* Frankie was pulled from the wreckage and taken to the hospital, healthy enough to live and serve another day of his sentence, though he walked with a nasty limp from then on.*

After that, cars at the prison had their batteries removed and gas tanks empty. This episode also marked the beginning of the end of the WSPAA, which boded well for the Bike Shop. The Bike Shop needed extra space and appreciated the WSPAA's handed-down paint booth. All of this made the Bike Shop happy and if the Bike Shop was happy, most everyone was happy.

22

Corrections Officer, Serial Killer, and Lifer

Robert Yates was a strange little guy, whom I never really noticed. A rookie guard low on the totem pole, he wasn't of much consequence to us prisoners. The sergeants and lieutenants, not to mention the captains, were of much more importance.

One night as I left the chow hall, Officer Yates, another officer and Sergeant Cross were just outside. I heard Yates say to Cross, "I want that one." Cross then said to me, "Hey, Kelley. Step over here for a shakedown." I didn't get what it was all about, but for Cross's sake, I stepped over and let Yates do a shakedown. Yates yelled that he had something. Sure enough, I had my sock half full of sugar for my cell partner, who had diabetes. He liked to keep sugar on-hand in case he had a blood sugar drop.

Yates got all excited and took my jacket and started going through it. It was a Vietnam jungle shirt, with four pockets. Low and behold, he finds one of those small spiral notebooks in one of the pockets and decides he needs to read the entries, looking for information on drug deals.

Well, Yates didn't find much in my notebook, or so it seemed until he came to a section with notes about a young couple killed up Mill Creek, east of Walla Walla. I was interested in this because I was always looking for new evidence to help me get a new trial—maybe this unsolved murder could shed light onto my wife's death. My deceased wife's boyfriend, Phillip Daniels, often took her up Mill Creek to have his way with her, or so I was told.

Having studied psychology for several years, I developed a knack of detecting anxiety in others. After reading my entry where I noted that the killer was possibly law enforcement or a correctional officer, I saw Yates get nervous. He began weaving back and forth, and seemed really confused all of the sudden. Exploiting my observation, right off I asked him what he was doing the day those kids were killed up Mill Creek. Yates actually stuttered in saying that he had nothing to do with those killings. Cross looked at him strangely and announced that the shakedown was over, and that I would get a citation for the sugar.

I headed one way and they went the other, Yates leaving the sock of sugar on the ground. I heard Cross tell Yates that he'd left his evidence back there. Yates obviously had no intention of citing me or turning in the report. He took the sugar, though, wrote up the incident, and then sent both to the trash bin.

Next time I saw Yates he was walking with my uncle Officer Cecil Hults. I said, Hey, Uncle Ces. How's it going? Then, just for larks, I asked, Say, Yates. What is your blood type?

Yates said to Uncle Ces (the whole Bike Shop referred to him as Uncle Ces), Hults, he's harassing me. Let's write him up. Uncle Ces told him, We got work to do. Let's go. They left me there.

Shortly thereafter Yates quit working at the prison. I didn't hear anything more about him for a while and then one day the Spokane paper announced that it found a serial killer: Robert Yates. He was sentenced to death. I always thought it was ironic that the only infraction I received in ten years was written by a serial killer.

23

The Killing of Ricky Johnson

Ricky came to prison via Monroe, the juvenile facility, where he was a sort of tough guy. He showed up at Walla Walla in his early-20s, about five feet, ten inches tall, 140 pounds, with long, blonde-hair and . . . you can probably see where this will end. Right away Ricky was raped, and it was obvious there would be more assaults. Somehow Ricky struck up a friendship with a wiry, older Mexican guy, who was a Bike Shop member. Ricky saw the advantage of going from being routinely raped by anyone, to being a pressure punk to one guy, especially since his protector was in a powerful club.

This arrangement lasted for a while and then the protector finished his sentence and was ready to go home. An arrangement was struck with Ricky's three roommates, all Bike Shop members, who swore to let Ricky live with them and also to protect him. All went well until Ricky got busted for a small amount of weed, sending him to segregation for two weeks. There he met Johnny, also in segregation for drugs, and a Bike Shop member. For whatever reason, my theory being that Johnny had a ready supply of drugs, Ricky and Johnny reached an agreement and Ricky gave sexual favors to Johnny while in segregation. Ricky gave a little ass for a good supply of drugs and maybe it seemed like a good deal for him; maybe even Ricky had started to like the gay lifestyle. After segregation, Ricky moved in with Johnny and his other cell partners, who right off took a dislike to Ricky. For the time, though, Johnny was in charge of the cell.

Unfortunately for Ricky the conditions of his living arrangement changed from his first relationship. With the old guy, all Ricky had to do was give up favors at night. Now Ricky was in a violent living situation, forced to wear women's underwear and use makeup. Of course, Ricky tried to get back to his old cell, but Johnny said "no" and Johnny had enough power to make it so. Johnny started making Ricky wear blouses and referred to him as his "bitch" in public. This all grated on Ricky, because it was taking the situation too far; Ricky wasn't gay or a transvestite, and all of this was making it appear otherwise.

For the Bike Shop, this was getting a little uncomfortable as well. Johnny was getting away with stuff that wasn't tolerated by other Bike Shop members, and so Johnny was pressured to get rid of Ricky. When the discussion took place, Johnny was high on heroin and said a few things he shouldn't have about the kid, and it seemed to everyone that Johnny was way too fond of Ricky.

My analysis was that if Johnny didn't want to get rid of Ricky, then Ricky should have PC'd up (gone into protective custody), but Ricky knew if he did, he would be labeled a rat. Then the rapes would continue while in PC, only the culprit would be lots of different guys. Ultimately Ricky opted to ride things out with Johnny; Ricky only had a couple more years in prison.

Johnny was outraged when he learned that some of his Bike Shop brothers tried to convince Ricky to opt for PC. Possibly the situation could have remained on simmer for the rest of Ricky's sentence, but it didn't. Shortly thereafter, Ricky was found on A tier in his cell, hanging with his hands tied behind his back. Many, including me, thought it strange that his hands were tied, but prosecuting attorney Arthur Eggers and Sergeant Morgan, the eight wing sergeant, agreed that if you untied his hands, it looked like just another suicide. Ricky went home in a box. Justice was later served as Johnny was stabbed in the eight wing shower, after being thrown out of the Bike Shop.

All of this was really unnecessary. Ricky was not an escape risk, and he wasn't violent, so he never should have been sent to Walla Walla. The powers that sent him to the penitentiary had to know how this would end. They may not have known he would end up dead, but they had to know that he would be sexually assaulted. That was a no-brainer.

24

Ethan Hoffman

In the late 1970s, Spalding called me into his office. He told me he had these two crazy reporters who wanted to roam around the joint without officer protection. Ethan Hoffman and John McCoy, both journalists, got permission to interview and take pictures of inmates at Walla Walla, after I assured Spalding that the Bike Shop would watch over them. The Bike Shop thought this would be great publicity for the work we were doing, and Hoffman assured us that his pictures of the shop would be flattering. We told all shop members to fully cooperate with him.

Generally, a shop member accompanied Hoffman around the prison, keeping the dings from interrupting his work. Some of the stuff Hoffman wanted to cover was frowned upon by other prisoners, and so I was sent to accompany him in the event he encountered a non-cooperative inmate. My job was to explain to resisting prisoners that this was important for the bike shop and emphasize that the shop would really appreciate their cooperation. This approach seemed to open a lot of doors, literally.

One day Hoffman was taking pictures in the eight wing shower. Hoffman showed up about shower time and started to set up for pictures. There was a big outcry by those in the shower, with lots of cusswords invoked. Hoffman was a bit taken aback, but after some words of encouragement, from myself, everyone agreed that allowing pictures was beneficial to all.

In truth, most inmates were happy to talk to Hoffman and have their picture taken, and Hoffman went to great lengths to ensure that no pictures would negatively impact a person's sentence. Many of his pictures are here in this book. I cannot thank his sister enough for giving me license to share them here.

25

The Killing of a Car Club (WSPAA) Member

One guy's position in the prison social strata was so insignificant that I can't recall his name, though I remember his story. He had been a member of the WSPAA for several years.

By way of background, the WSPAA always wanted to have some clout, be of some consequence, in the prison power structure, but it never even got close. At one time their plan to amass power was to take over the Alcoholics Anonymous (AA) clubhouse. Since many of the WSPAA members were also AA members, the WSPAA already wielded some significant power in AA, but they wanted more. The AA had a pretty good income from gambling. Once the clubhouse doors were closed to the 12-stepping drunks, it served nicely as a casino.

One particular day a WSPAA member was playing dominos with Boots, an AA member in his late 60s or 70s who was extremely tall and thin. On account of Boots' perceived weaknesses (being old and frail), the WSPAA member thought he could cheat, without repercussion. In fact, many overlooked similar Bike Shop member cheats, but the difference was in the prison power structure: The Bike Shop had power, while the WSPAA did not.

That day Boots outright called the WSPAA on his cheat and was smacked down for doing so. It was obvious that Boots could not take this guy in a fist fight, so after a few words the WSPAA member left and went back to his clubhouse, feeling pretty good about himself. He had put AA on notice that the WSPAA was moving in on their power.

What the WSPAA member did not take into account was that Boots had money and was well-liked, so it was easy for Boots to hire a hit on the

WSPAA cheat. And it was just Boots' luck that one of the most dangerous inmates had just been released from segregation (again). Every time this inmate was released from segregation, someone was stabbed within a week or so.

A little later the WSPAA member came back to the AA clubhouse to gamble. As he entered the room, someone stepped out from behind the door and stabbed him once in the chest. The WSPAA member turned and ran toward his clubhouse, which was a good half block away, collapsing at his clubhouse door. Most of the prison, staff and inmate alike, knew who the assassin was, but no charges were ever filed. There is a big difference between knowing and having proof beyond a reasonable doubt.

Bike Shop showing the author's 1937 Harley-Davidson, serial number 37UL2105. Governor Ray looks on. Restored by Bike Shop member Richard Anderson. Photo supplied by James Spalding, Director of Corrections.

26

The Killing of Richard Anderson

Richard was a bike shop brother, as well as an excellent body and fender man. His paint jobs were show quality and he loved painting custom motorcycles.

His death was senseless. It started this way: at lunch in the chow hall we were having spaghetti. The line the bike shop used ran out of spaghetti, so a shop brother told a guy in the other line to put some spaghetti on his plate. This guy in the other line, a lifer ding, was good friends of the biker, or so we all thought. But the biker's request came to argument, including words like punk and it's going in your ass.

After exchanging words, the lifer kid left, and our shop brother waited for him as he came out the cafeteria door. In the ensuing fight, our brother had the best of the lifer kid and beat him pretty soundly.

Previously, the lifer president announced that he would not allow anyone to beat up a club member, and now he was in a tough spot. He either had to follow through with consequences or back off and let it slide. Compromising, the lifer president arranged for a rematch fight at the lifer clubhouse, and this time it was even worse for the lifer ding. The ding got really hammered by my shop brother, who was the older of the two, but also tough as nails.

After that, the bike shop figured it was settled, though it was not. As consequence for beating a club member, the lifer president ordered a hit on me, since I was the Bike Shop vice president. I suppose the fact that the member who beat up the lifer kid (twice) was my best friend had also pushed me front and center. Besides, I was considered a softer target than my bike shop friend.

It was my practice back then to return to my eight wing cell block, alone, at 8:30 pm. However, this night a small, internal voice kept telling me to go back to the cell block at 8:45 pm instead, alongside my shop brothers, which is what I ultimately did.

Now in the bike shop there are three guys who really look alike: me, Richard and Keith. Richard went back to eight wing by himself at 8:30 pm, was mistaken for me and was killed. After Richard's death, the hit was supposedly done. However, Warren Halverson, a respected Lifer whose life I saved while working in the kitchen, kindly informed me that the hit was still out on me, and to watch myself.

It would have been easy as vice president to go to the bike shop and tell my brothers about this threat, effectively declaring war on the Lifers. Somehow, I just couldn't do that; I felt too terrible about Richard getting killed in my place. Declaring war would have put other shop brothers' lives in jeopardy, so I decided to handle it myself, as I tend to do.

First, I got my good friend in the machine shop, Jim Fogle, to make me a T-shirt of small lock washers. At the time, I was taking college classes at the education building. That building had some dangerous blind corners, but I didn't just want to drop out of the program; to me that just was not an option. Instead I put on my armored T-shirt and prayed I would make it to and from school safely.

One night coming back from the education building, a lifer jumped out and rushed toward me with a shank. I dropped him with a side kick to the knee, then felt a pain in my back followed by a second blow to the back. A second lifer had surfaced, stabbing me. I whirled around and rammed a pencil though this second lifer's mouth and cheek. This stopped the attack, and I watched him run out of the building. There were three BPFU brothers watching. I informed them they didn't see anything, because if they had they would be dead tomorrow. I didn't want this little attack to get publicity and make its way back to the bike shop, because it could start a war. However, I knew this probably would not be the end of the squabble. I was left with bad bruises on my back, but no puncture wounds. Neither of the injured Lifers went to the hospital right away, though the one who got the pencil through his cheek later went due to a bad infection.

I stopped by the Control Room and told the Lt. in charge that I would be taking the 9:00 pm count in the kitchen, which was something bike club members often did. I needed to talk to St. Peter, a good friend of mine and a Lifer.

I went in the kitchen and told St. Peter what happened. He surprised me when he announced there was nothing that he could do to help me. I heard rumors that the bike shop and the lifers club had pistols, but, as vice president of the shop, I had never seen a pistol or heard any serious talk that the shop actually had one. I told St. Peter that the next time I got jumped I would have a pistol and use it, resulting in a prison-wide, serious-as-a-heart-attack lockdown. This got St. Peter's attention, since lockdown is absolutely no fun. He said, I will take care of it; it's over. You've got my word. The Secret Police never brought any follow up information on a hit on me to my attention. In fact, true to St. Peter's word, that really was the end of it; there was no more violence between the bike shop and the lifers after that.

27

Superintendent Larry Kinchole

I worked closely with Larry while at Walla Walla. He was a former military officer and hadn't been contaminated by the politics of Washington's Department of Corrections. That made him fair and not afraid to do what was right, rather than what was politically correct. Later, after I was released from prison and while he was superintendent of maximum security in Alaska, he flew down (on his own dime) to testify at my motion hearing for a new trial. Two things stood out in his testimony:

1. If there was one success story while he had been in Corrections, I was it; and
2. While he was Associate Superintendent at Walla Walla, he would check the charts to see where I would be that day, because he knew that there wouldn't be trouble in that sector.

After he testified, we talked and reminisced about our first meeting. He said that when he first talked to Superintendent Spalding, he was told to keep an eye on me. Spalding described me as tall with long hair, and vice-president of the bike shop. Larry remembered walking into the bike shop for the first time, where he found Kenny Atuga kicked back on two legs of a chair, with Tony Wheat chatting with him (both non-members of the bike shop). When he saw me walk in, he thought to himself that I must have been in the military, because I walked in perfect military fashion. Also, as I came in all the chit chat stopped, and Kenny put the other two legs of his chair down. Larry saw that everyone got down to business immediately. Larry remembered thinking that I was obviously in charge of the bike shop.

Larry asked me why the shop allowed Richard Anderson to be killed, without retaliation. I answered honestly that the shop president responded in the way he thought was best for the shop. Larry asked me what I would have done, had I been in charge. I answered that I wouldn't second-guess the president's decision. Larry then asked whether the decision was made because the shop just didn't have the power to retaliate.

I couldn't let that one go, and I took the bait. I told him that the shop was never scared at any time, and it had the will and means to take out the lifer leadership, had they been asked to do so by the shop president. Larry asked how we could have done that: we were outnumbered four to one at the time.

I told Larry that after Richard was killed, St. Peter came to me and wanted to know what I wanted to do with the lifer leadership. Maybe you understand what that meant . . . at the time lifer leadership was bringing a lot of heat to the lifer members. To St. Peter this created a problem, because as a lifer, the extra attention hindered his plans for his next escape. St. Peter told me that he and some other lifers were ready to deal with the problem themselves: an uprising among the members. I told St. Peter that the shop's president had already handled it, and that's where we stood. As I told Larry all this background, I could tell he understood what had really happened. The shop wasn't grasping for power, but rather was responding to a power imbalance within and among the prison's clubs.

While head of the motor pool, we worked often on Larry's son's Volkswagen Bug. Through this and other interactions, I got to know his family fairly well. I was invited to their home a few times and I remember, particularly, that his daughter had two cute bunnies—one named Sunrise and one named Tequila.

28

The Killing of The Monk

The Monk was a strange little guy in his middle-40s with a bushy afro and a fairly bushy beard. He belonged to the BPFU and never bothered anyone, though he did have three pressing problems:

1. He liked pruno;
2. He didn't make his own pruno;
3. He stole pruno.

The penalty for theft was death. Though this seems extreme, remember that in prison the abnormal is normal and normal is abnormal.

Because of his intimate, long-standing relationship with pruno, The Monk developed an uncanny smell for it. He could sense its presence from a mile away, it seemed. Unsurprisingly, he discovered a pruno stash and was in the habit of sampling it on a regular basis. It didn't take long before his indiscretion was discovered and he was given a severe roughing-up as a warning for his theft; under prison rules, beatings didn't require approval before administering. But for a hard-core addict like the monk, the threat of a beating wasn't enough to get him off the sauce; he kept sampling and was again caught.

The pruno entrepreneur, a white guy, came to the Bike Shop requesting permission to kill the monk. The Bike Shop turned the matter over to the BPFU, since The Monk was black. A meeting between the prison powers (BPFU, the Bike Shop, and the Lifers Club) took place in the big yard, where it was safe for all to attend and talk. The pruno entrepreneur made his case, demanding the death penalty. Some didn't like such severe punishment over stealing a bit of pruno, but still felt it was fair when applied to someone stealing drugs. It was a tenuous situation: if the BPFU said, "no death penalty" while everyone else voted for the death penalty, then a war could result.

Ultimately a BPFU member suggested that they let The Monk kill himself. All they had to do was spike the pruno with battery acid and when the monk drank the stolen liquid, he would kill himself. The BPFU even volunteered the battery acid.

Sure enough, The Monk couldn't stay away from the pruno and sure enough he drank more than he should have. I learned that the symptoms of someone who drinks battery acid include:

1. Lost control of bowels;
2. Lost control of bladder;
3. Nose running out of control, resulting in looking like a dog with distemper; and
4. Unsteady gait.

The Monk developed these symptoms and went to the hospital; the hospital couldn't figure out what happened. The last time I saw The Monk he was in the control room, meeting with BJ Rhay about his health concerns. The monk was not talking very well, smelling really bad, and staggering. He died shortly thereafter.

29

The Attack on Jimmy

Jimmy was a bike shop brother repeatedly accused of murdering other inmates, but always found not guilty by juries. In his early 20s and very muscular, Jimmy was a brother you could really count on.

Jimmy worked in the kitchen, which was mainly run by the BPFU. Jimmy got into it with a black brother known as The Cannibal, a ding.[46] As a result of their argument, Jimmy beat up The Cannibal and the BPFU wanted war. The next Friday Jimmy, Flint, Pineapple, Blinky (all bike shop brothers) and I were going down Blood Alley, right past the BPFU clubhouse.

As we walked down the breezeway with our recently acquired rounds of sodas, we saw The Cannibal with his back against the brick wall of the cell block. When we walked past, he let out a roar and then stabbed Jimmy above the heart, downward. Later we learned that the knife missed Jimmy's heart by 1/4 of an inch. Next Pineapple pulled out his nunchucks and beat The Cannibal away from Jimmy. The Cannibal ran into the BPFU clubhouse, screaming and bleeding from his numerous head wounds, shouting that the bike shop attacked him. A bunch of BPFU members came running out of their clubhouse and Flint pulled out a Roman short sword and he and Pineapple chased the BPFU guys back into their clubhouse. The door swung out, me and Blinky, in his 40s but one of the toughest guys I have ever known, ran up and held the door shut while Pineapple and Flint rushed Jimmy to the hospital.

---

46 When he was arrested, he was found with a head and fingers in a brown sack he was carrying, and he had been chewing on the fingers.

It sounded like a hornet's nest inside the clubhouse. On the count of three and after seeing our brothers safely out of Blood Alley, Blinky and I raced off. I was thrown by the door toward six wing. I raced into six wing and went to Jimmy Fogle's cell while Blinky raced to the bike shop to warn the brothers that a war had started—and the bike shop was part of it. After a meeting of the bike shop and BPFU leaders, it was decided that a ding like The Cannibal was no reason to go to war. Jimmy survived, but later both he and Flint left the bike shop. Upon release, Jimmy was haunted by the murders he committed and eventually he killed himself.

30

Richard Morgan, Secretary of Corrections, Eight Wing Sergeant

October 20, 2016, I had a chance to interview Dick Morgan. We go back a long time, to when he was my cell block sergeant during the late 1970s. At that time, the bike shop controlled the prison, and eight wing in particular. Many a night when the 9:00 pm lockdown was minutes away with half the wing still wandering about, Sergeant Morgan would ask a shop brother to give him a hand getting the place locked down. It only took one shop member to shout, "In your cells NOW," and the doors would start clanging shut.

I always felt Dick treated us right and considered him more of a friend than a guard, though Dick always put business first. I feel comfortable referring to him as Dick, in spite of his former high station as Secretary of Corrections.

Dick grew up in Walla Walla (the city, not the prison) and while between jobs, he had to submit some job applications to keep his unemployment checks rolling in. To his surprise, one application actually panned out: The Department of Corrections at Washington State Penitentiary in Walla Walla offered him a job. Never imagining that he would spend his career there, Dick took the job, though his dream and goal was to become a lawyer for underdogs, along the lines of Clarence Darrel or F. Lee Bailey. I think that tells you a lot about what kind of guy Dick is.

Well, with a job offer and all, Dick found himself working at the Walla Walla. His first day on-shift was in eight wing. "I remember walking into the wing and the stench was overwhelming. I couldn't really put a handle on it. Walking around back to work the showers, I discovered that inmates had been shitting in the shower and I had the luck to step in some of it."

With his career off to an interesting start, he endured. He remembered working in the segregation unit, overseeing some of the worst prisoners, one of which was The Cannibal. Dick remembers that every time he walked by The Cannibal's cell, The Cannibal would say, You sure enough have some good teeth. Creepy as hell and shades of Hannibal Lector, if you ask me. After stabbing bike shop member Jimmy Carlyle, The Cannibal was sent to see Dr. Hunter and, like many before him, The Cannibal never returned. Die Gutte Sturmbannfuher[47] Hunter had a certain way with the mentally ill.

Dick also remembers a little fellow named Terry, with light yellow, almost white, hair and a slim, 5'10" build. Terry was a wannabe for bike shop membership, and he saw himself as a tough guy. However, Terry's concurrent favor for the gay lifestyle left his dream of bike shop membership unrealized.

Terry decided that his tough guy image would be enhanced and embraced by the prison population, if only he shanked a guard. Cautious by nature, Terry decided to test that theory by using a rubber knife on a practice run. Yes—you read that right. A rubber hunting knife, to be exact, that looked just like the real thing. Dick was on one of the tiers, sitting on a stool, when Terry charged up and started stabbing him with this rubber knife. He remembers, It scared the shit out of me and haunted me for years. Had it been a real knife, I'd be dead.

Instead of becoming known as a tough guy, Terry became known as a crazy gay guy, and his experiment in shanking Dick earned him a sound beating by bike shop members. You can't attack the eight wing sergeant without permission from the shop, and they are never granting permission. Later Ray caught Terry in the shower and had his way with him. Eventually Terry got transferred to The Farm and ran off, after getting raped in the movie hall.

Dick could never forget the 4:00 pm count that went on for several

47 Translated to English as "the good assault unit leader" (German World War I title).

hours, always coming up with one extra prisoner. Of course, the error was coming out of eight wing. Dick said, "For the third and fourth count, they went around and checked every single cell, and we still always came up with the same count, and the institution continued to be one over every time."

The next time the Control Room ordered a card check. In each wing they had a card for every cell, with pictures of those who live in that cell. Bingo. They found four men in a cell, with one of the guys not matching the card for that cell, and one man is missing from the cell according to the card. The kitchen, where the missing inmate worked, was called. Sure enough—the missing inmate was in the kitchen working. Now they had their extra guy. The control room called and told the eight wing staff to not open the cell, and that the shift lieutenant was on the way. Turns out the extra guy hadn't been sentenced by any court. In fact, he had no record at all. He came into the prison with a performing theater group, and fell in love with an inmate, on a previous visit. It was supposed to work out that the inmate from eight wing would hide in the kitchen and not be counted, meanwhile the free world man would be taking his place in the eight wing cell. A beautiful, romantic night was never realized, cut short when the kitchen worker got counted.

Johnny, a former Bike Shop member, ran a porn racket and had been warned to vacate eight wing ASAP. Dick remembers standing at the gate when Johnny came walking up with a towel wrapped around him, with gaping, bleeding head wounds, and blood dripping down his legs. I learned later that Johnny had been attacked while in the shower. Dick asked what happened and he said, "Nothing. I'm OK." By that time, Johnny was shaking and nearly in shock. Dick hollered for a gurney and tried to plug the holes in his torso with his fingers. Johnny did survive and did get out of eight wing.

One day Sergeant Wayne Helgeson called the control room while Dick was working. An inmate named Childress was on the floor in eight wing, bleeding badly, with the fingers of an EMT on his chest, attempting to stem the bleeding. Dick recalls looking at him, then saying, "He's dead."

In spite of the constant danger, there were lighter moments. Dick Morgan remembers an initiation rite for new guards: removing the eight wing sallie port door, which just sat on its hinges. If it wasn't locked, it was easily removed and hidden, which caused new officers much pain. He also remembers a 1977 lockdown. The inmates were hollering about killing someone if they got another TV dinner with the chicken missing. It seems Able Gonzales, a guard, was taking the chicken.

Dick Morgan remembers a night lieutenant who was a bit compulsive, to state it mildly. Before this lieutenant would go off-shift, he sharpened all his pencils and lain them out in length order on his desk. After leaving for the day, another guard would put one or two out of length order, just to drive the compulsive guard crazy.

No doubt it was a tough job. Dick remembers the most frustrating thing about working at Walla Walla was the lack of supervision and lack of direction from above. Memos ran the institution, and every week policy changed, and changed again . . . and changed again.

Dick Morgan was the last head of the Department of Corrections to have gotten a start in the 1970s. Dick's hard work, alongside Jim Spalding, Larry Kinchole, Lieutenant Dodd, Captain Talbott, Lieutenant Thompson, Parley Edwards, Officer Rob Hults, Officer Tim Snell, Superintendent John Lampert, Lieutenant R. Mason, these latter four were original members of the Dodd Squad, along with a few others, changed Walla Walla from a killing field to a safe and secure institution, both for staff and inmates. Appointment of leaders completely inexperienced in institutions and corrections resulted in many, many deaths and assaults.

31

Cadillac Brown, Heroin Supply, and the Killing of McCoy

Lots of inmates resorted to prescription drugs in coping with their time behind bars. If you could convince a doctor, prescription drugs made your time there quite bearable, and the drugs flowed quite freely for those with the right approach. Sometimes inmate complaints to get these drugs were psychological, sometimes physical—whatever it took to keep the good drugs rolling in. Then in early 1972, shortly after I got there, the well ran dry after a sit-down strike, orchestrated by the inmates demanding changes in hospital health care staff. The strike resulted in resignation by much of the medical staff, with a new doctor who took over inmate medical treatment. This doctor was appalled at the number of prescription drugs, many habit-forming, inmates had been dispensed for years. The result was a serious curtail in prescription drugs, which was not exactly what the strike organizers were looking for.[48] This, combined with the advent of the RGC, open visiting, and outside phone calls, resulted in a tremendous illegal prison drug trade, the flow of which was overseen by an inmate named Cadillac Brown, a member of the BPFU.[49]*

Cadillac Brown was the heroin kingpin at Walla Walla. Not only was he on the retail side, but he was also the major supplier. True to form, Cadillac was in prison on a narcotics charge, and after hitting the prison he kept right on working in his field. After getting to the penitentiary, Cadillac was assigned to work the prison switchboard, where he could

---

48 Murray at 54.
49 Murray at 55.

make unlimited and unregulated phone calls whenever he wanted. He got this job because the BPFU was in charge of the phone's office, while the bike shop was in charge of the inmate store. Employees at each office reported to the respective club, not the prison's staff. Soon after, heroin started flowing into the penitentiary from all directions: through mail, through visitors, through milk cans from the dairy, through sides of beef, through corrupt staff, through prison volunteers, and, some said, through bike parts purchased by the bike shop.[50]

Some BPFU presidents tried to convince others that the bike shop was bringing in all the heroin, but that was just not true. One BPFU president actually testified secretly (well, it would have been a secret, but the Secret Police had gotten to some high-up administration people) that the bikers were bringing in heroin through the down tubes of the Harley Davidson Sportsters motorcycles, "the ones where the gas tank was part of the frame." The Harley Davidson Motor Company testified that they had never made a motorcycle that had the gas tank as part of the frame. However, a former BPFU president pointed the finger at the bike shop, saying that in Sportsters there was lots of room for packing in cannabinol and heroin.[51]

I'm not saying that the bike shop was a bunch of angels, but the fact remained that the bike shop was not bringing in drugs on a large scale. The truth was the real drug supply network was run by a prison sergeant. This sergeant would bring in heroin, in large quantities, for Cadillac, with little or no fear of getting caught. This sergeant went too far, however, and a new prison policy was implemented. Previously if a guard got caught packing in drugs, the penalty was firing and the matter would be kept hush-hush, with no charges filed. This sergeant, who was making maybe $20,000 a year from working at the prison, could make ten times that amount supplementing his income by bringing in drugs. Given that the risk of getting caught carried very little penalty other than losing a low-paying job, it was a fair gamble. Unfortunately for

---

50 Murray at 55.
51 Murray at 165.

this sergeant things changed, and when he was caught, for the first time prison personnel were charged in Superior Court on felony counts for supplying drugs.

In the end the bikers never brought in heroin, at least not that I knew of. Individual bikers, not the shop, would buy heroin from Cadillac for resale. The BPFU also bought from Cadillac, and so biker and BPFU members would be the retailers for heroin in the prison. Others brought in dope or heroin, sold it, and generally paid their taxes.

McCoy was a sharp little weasel. He had worked a deal where he would get a supply of heroin from the BPFU (which was untaxed and therefore illegal under the prisoner's justice system) and sell it to others. Of course, it takes no time for this to get around the prison; dopers can never keep a secret. So, the bike shop had a chat with McCoy and it was all friendly, with no threats, and McCoy was told to pay taxes or get out of business. Well, McCoy thought since he had become such a good businessman for the BPFU, that they would protect him from the bike shop. In reality, the shop had no intentions of hurting McCoy, rather he needed to watch out for the BPFU.

Cadillac was informed, through the BPFU, that McCoy was not paying his taxes. This was discovered in March 1976, when a biker saw McCoy selling heroin. McCoy was given a chance to play by the rules and pay his taxes, but he didn't and so a biker killed him, claiming self-defense.[52] Cadillac agreed to take care of the problem, or talk to McCoy at some point. However, Cadillac knew who really ran the prison (the Bike Shop) and he panicked, instead paying a biker to take care of the problem immediately. After all, McCoy was not in a position to threaten Cadillac, but merely a drug dealer, like a hundred other prisoners. Of course, with such a power position, Cadillac was also a target for up-and-coming competitors, and when competition arose, Cadillac checked into protective custody. Two other prisoners named Wally Bishop and Bud Ferguson then ran the prison drug trade until Bud was knifed, crippled, and checked into protective custody. This knifing was not over drugs,

---

52 Murray at 118.

but rather a love triangle over a red-haired kid. Wally also got out of the business at that point and went in with the bike shop. In the end, whoever had the best visiting room packer generally had a corner on the drug trade.*

As with any retail enterprise, drug sales required payment, and payment required collection efforts; the bike shop was the recognized enforcement body for the prison. One corrections officer remembered being warned by the bike shop that the guards shouldn't be surprised when they saw a lot of black eyes, because it was debt collection season.[53] The bike shop also served as the taxing authority for all dope sales, enforcing it in straightforward but violent ways: smashing the tax-evader's hand in the clubhouse vice grip.[54] We liked to call this vice grip the "lie detector." If non-compliance continued to be a problem, of course the next level of punishment was death.[55]

---

53 Murray at 117.
54 Id.
55 Id.

32

Drugs, Drugs and More Drugs

Lieutenant Dodd recalls that by the middle of 1971, drug debts had gotten so big that a tier was opened in the segregation unit for drug debtors, with a new category of protective custody just for the big-time drug dealers. As it happened, once someone new took over prison drug sales, the old sellers had to check in with the new chief or be assaulted and sometimes killed. Sometimes the best snitches were drug dealers who wanted the competition locked up, but what comes around goes around and so soon the snitch was in the sites of new, wannabe competitors.* But even better than competitors, the most reliable snitches were just inmates, tired of the violence and wanting it to end.*

The solution, in part, to the increased need for protective custody was to send more of these inmates to the farm or Minimum-Security Building (MSB). Lieutenant Dodd remembers three MSB inmates assigned to a dairy crew, when one turned up missing. Upon searching the west field where cows were grazing, Dodd found a half pair of dentures and a lot of blood. Following the blood trail, Dodd found a half-buried body. Then another MSB inmate, who supposedly escaped, was found a couple of days later, hanging by a logging chain at an outside construction site. Dodd was skeptical it was a suicide.*

From Lieutenant Dodd's perspective, finding drugs in a shakedown was no big deal. In fact, competitors in the drug trade found it easy to get an edge on their competition by simply ratting them out. As a result, Dodd was making so many busts that the RGC complained to prison management.* Known as one to never back down, Dodd recalls learning that sometimes discretion is better than getting your ass handed to you.

In late 1973 Dodd was orienting a new officer, Richard Mason, and the two walked down Blood Alley. The BPFU clubhouse generally had a doorman who warned when officers were coming down the breezeway, but that day there was no doorman. Before any possibility of warning the clubhouse, Dodd and the new officer gently barged into the BPFU office to find inmates selling shots of heroin. An exceptionally large prisoner named Louis Jackson immediately scooped up the three heroin-filled needles and some cash in his left hand, and then Dodd grabbed his left forearm and ordered him to stand for a shakedown. He raised his left hand, forcing Dodd to his tiptoes to maintain the grip. Louis looked directly into Dodd's eyes and said he was refusing and that as soon as he flushed what was in his hand, he would go to lockup. Dodd and the officer went to the control room, where Jackson soon reported and was placed in segregation.* Officer Mason commented to Dodd, "I thought you never backed down." As everyone knows, never can be a long time and not always workable.

During the early 1970s the drug situation at the prison was out of control, by any estimation. Superintendent Rhay refused to promote sergeants off the promotion roster, as required by policy. When the state opened the sergeant's exam in 1973, there were twelve sergeant positions unfilled.*Sergeants were used to backfill officer positions, and so, staff going home sick during mid-shift became a crisis: there was no one to fill the post. To get basement checks in the evenings, the control room officer sat guard, while the cell lieutenants did the checks. Unit officers did the cell security checks (i.e., checking the bars, floors, walls and ceiling for possible escape attempts). Cell shakedowns were few and far between, because they just didn't have the manpower.* As a result, staff turnover was high[56]* and morale was subterranean, with no staff wanting to assume responsibility for any prison function.* Meanwhile, the hospital was dispensing most anything the inmates requested, and lots of those inmates were merely mouthing (i.e., not swallowing) their medications,

---

56 In 1972 the prison population got as low as 42 while the murder rate just kept escalating.

later selling them. Also, drugs were starting to flood in through the more open visiting policy.*

One time Dodd stopped an inmate for a shakedown and instead the inmate took off running. Dodd chased him to the TV rooms where the inmate, taking out a bag of marijuana, emptied it on the floor, while other inmates picked it up and ate it.* When two inmates took over the hospital and held nurses hostage in 1974, the first thing they did was break into the pharmacy and throw all kinds of pills out the windows, where inmates picked them up and ate them.* Later Dodd picked up a comatose inmate and took him to the hospital for an overdose. The physician's assistant gave the inmate a shot of Narcan and the inmate immediately sat up, hollering, "You ruined a perfectly good high," while taking a swing at the physician's assistant.* A day later, Dodd found inmates had removed a manhole cover and were retrieving bottled drugs that had made their way into a storm drain.*

Balloons were often used to smuggle drugs into the prison. Once, the engineering department opened a manhole connected to the visiting room toilet, and found it almost three feet deep in balloons, most of which had been packaging for smuggled drugs. Another time a sewer line plugged up and the parking lot flooded with balloons.*

When they found manpower for it, the prison organized cell shakedowns, and Lieutenant Dodd was selected to head the crew. When Lieutenant Dodd's shakedown crew entered a cell block, the first inmate to see them yelled, Dodd Squad! and then the toilets started flushing. When they had manning, these crews were known as Goon Squad, though Interstate Tommy rebranded them Dodd Squad while I was there. Eventually inmates stored their drugs, and occasionally a weapon, on the small ledge outside their cell doors. The Dodd Squad developed a system of searching a cell, with the four-member squad each manning a quarter of the cell, while the first to enter immediately went to the toilet to prevent the flushing of drugs. When an inmate threw his drugs off of F-tier, one of the Dodd Squad members swung over the tiers to pick up the drugs before a couple of inmates got to them.*

Dodd developed a sense for whom to shakedown: those who were more interested in him, than he was in them. One day an RGC representative and prisoner, who was apparently trying to get a handle on snitching in the prison, said that he would escort Dodd as he walked through the prison population, to ensure that no one snitched. As they walked, Dodd came across a prisoner who definitely looked more interested in Dodd than Dodd was in him. Dodd doubled back to surprise the prisoner and told him to stand for a shakedown. Immediately putting his hands under the prisoner's arms, Dodd found a shank, and his fellow officer took the inmate down, where he found another shank. Dodd turned to the RGC representative and said, loudly, "Thanks for the tip!" The RGC representative backpedaled and said, "You are trying to get me killed." After that Dodd didn't have any more RGC escorts.*

Dodd found that after the Dodd Squad had been around for a while, it started losing its effectiveness; everywhere they went, prisoners would warn others by yelling, "Dodd Squad!" and the shakedown would lose its surprise advantage. One day Dodd decided to wait until dinner was called, and then close the tier and do a cell-by-cell search. There were tons of extra (unauthorized) linens, as well as a paper cutter blade, two homemade shanks, four or five needles with homemade syringes, three stolen radios[57], two radios with seals gone[58], and some unidentified pills. All of this was loaded into a large laundry cart, and they took it to the shift lieutenant's office, where they wrote up four cells for infractions.*

Once a Dodd Squad attempted to do a cell shakedown in the MSB. Upon arriving, Dodd spoke with the MSB lieutenant, who was not happy to see them and who provided them with a key that didn't fit the padlocks securing the cells. The squad's request to cut the locks was denied, and so the squad arranged to come back for their search of two cells when the MSB inmates returned from their workday. Meanwhile the inmates in those two cells got word of the search and simply walked away after their workday, while other MSB inmates, entering via a vent hole, cleared their cells of any contraband.* The next time the Dodd Squad ventured over

57 All inmate radios had their serial numbers recorded so they could track them if they were stolen. Inmates weren't allowed to sell or trade their radios.
58 Radios with the seals broken usually meant that the radio had been dismantled and was being used to hide and store all manner of illegal paraphernalia, like guns or drugs.

to the MSB, an inmate shouted "Dodd Squad!" Dodd walked into the sergeant's office and said hello, while two members walked around the outside of the building, picking up the contraband being thrown out the windows.*

Walk aways were frequent at the MSB, and therefore not unusual; in fact, Lieutenant Dodd recalls that they were no big deal.* During one year in the 1970s there were more than 70 walk aways.* A state law at the time said that if a private citizen helped in the capture of an escaped felon, the citizen could claim a $25 reward. In 1972 Dodd went to collect three walk aways by going to a woman's house near the prison. The woman pointed to the back of her house, where three prisoners were running through the field, away from their would-be captors. When the prisoners heard gun fire and "Halt!" they stopped and put their hands up. The woman reminded them of her reward: three prisoners at $25 each equals $75. Other walk aways got drunk, took farm tractors joyriding, and generally raised hell before their capture.*

Lieutenant Dodd remembers learning about some quirks with qualifying for parole as a lifer. Generally, a life sentence was 20 years and an inmate was eligible for parole with a little over 13 years served. One inmate served just nine years, and this inmate was a big-time drug dealer with a poor behavioral record in prison. Dodd asked a 17-year Lifer why he hadn't gotten out on parole. He smiled and said he didn't have $25,000, otherwise he would have. Dodd talked to a couple of other Lifers and they told him the same thing was happening at other state institutions: life-sentence prisoners were buying parole.*

33

Prison Discipline

The prison had a disciplinary committee, presided over by Mr. Macklin, the Associate Superintendent, until he left in early 1971.* For discipline, Macklin would sentence inmates to ten days blackout, then twenty days segregation, followed by administrative segregation. Blackout meant moving to individual cells with solid doors and one window. The door was opened three times a day for food and then closed after the tray was picked up. The light switch was on the tier (i.e., outside the inmate's control). That discipline got an inmate's attention quickly, so long as the inmate was sane. However, it did not work with the mentally ill inmates, which was a problem since Walla Walla housed the state's mentally ill.*

When Rhay was warden, he would go into the prison once a week for interviews with inmates. The waiting room to see him was often full. However, after overhearing an inmate interview where Rhay hollered at an inmate, the inmates in the waiting room would often ask to go back to their cells. Though the wait was often months for an interview, nobody wanted to meet with Rhay when Rhay was upset. After a "loud" interview, Rhay would exit the interview room and, finding the waiting room empty, smile and leave.*

Snitches, though varying in their motives, always existed. Sometimes a snitch wasn't needed; staff could tell who dealt drugs by noting which cells were frequented by drug users. Other times, when making rounds, a guard walking past a cell would hear an inmate whisper a cell number. This told the guard that cell was a good target for a search.*

Jim Harvey became associate superintendent in 1974 and stayed until 1977. Jim Harvey was a guy that hated convicts, and that all guards adored--until he swiped their ladies. Administration hired him because they thought he had the skills to compensate for Rhay's shortcomings and, in the beginning, he was very by-the-book and no-nonsense.[59] He was hand-picked by the Director of the Division of Adult Corrections, Hal Bradley, after one of Bradley's visits to Walla Walla. Bradley could see that Rhay needed someone who could dispense more heavy-handed discipline, and Harvey seemed to fit the bill.[60] In the wake of increasing prisoner self-governance and Harvey's general distaste for prisoners, it shouldn't surprise anyone that Harvey grew to especially dislike the bike shop, since it was the most powerful club.

When Harvey became Associate Warden, I had a great job: running the eight wing mechanical room, located in the basement. I had my own room down there, and I could come and go most anytime. I was also the emergency electrician for the whole prison; any electrical problem during off-hours came to me. This amounted to a pretty enviable living and work set-up for me. The door to the mechanical room was on the west side of eight wing and the only way you could get to it is was by walking down "No Man's Land" between the wall and the west side of eight wing. I was rarely part of the general population at night, which meant a lot more freedom and safety.

By the time Harvey got there I was a fully-enfranchised member of the bike shop. One day Harvey called me in and told me that the only way I could stay in the eight wing mechanical room was if I would furnish him information on the bike shop. It took a millisecond for me to realize that he was asking me to be a snitch. I left his office and went to my room in the mechanical room and packed my stuff, turned off the fans and reported to my upstairs cell in eight wing. Harvey was furious and summoned me back into his office with instructions for me to go back to the mechanical room. I told him I would call my lawyer, Senator Herbert H. Friese, if he wanted to push the matter. After that I was on his shit list, but I couldn't have cared less. It turns out that Harvey was paying informants throughout

59 Murray at 84.
60 Murray at 83.

the prison with prison scrip. Through this prisoner-provided intelligence, Harvey learned about guns held in the Lifers clubhouse.[61]

About a month after Harvey's arrival in 1974, Dodd did a shakedown of a Chicano Club member. The first whispered words out of his mouth were, You cannot shake me down. I work for Mr. Harvey. Dodd proceeded with the shakedown and found a cigarette package with 180 mini beanies (e.g., speed). Dodd gently cuffed the prisoner and told him that it didn't matter who he worked for, if he packed drugs, he was going to segregation. The inmate told Dodd that he was going to be in trouble.*

The next day Dodd was called into Mr. Harvey's office. In his belligerent way, Harvey asked Dodd what he thought he was doing, locking up one of his snitches. Dodd replied that any inmate caught selling speed went to segregation. Harvey stormed out of the office, telling Lt Thompson (aka Hog Jowls) that Dodd was going to get hurt now, and Thompson needed to make sure that didn't happen.* Later a snitch came to Lieutenant Dodd requesting transfer to federal prison. If Dodd couldn't do it, he told Dodd that in a riot he (Dodd) would find himself in a real predicament Dodd responded, "Not really, they would have to kill me because I know all the rats!!"

Dodd and Thompson went to Thompson's office, where Thompson asked what that was all about. Dodd told him what happened and Thompson told Dodd to stay out of Harvey's way. Two weeks later Dodd went back into Harvey's office. Harvey then told Dodd how pleased he was that his snitch had been busted. I guess it had impressed the rest of the inmates when that snitch was busted, so it increased the credibility of the snitch among inmates. This, in turn, improved the quality of information the snitch was able to give Harvey. In the end, Dodd and Harvey seemed to work well together, though Harvey and Rhay always seemed to be at odds.*

One day Harvey asked Dodd to transport a prisoner in a single-engine aircraft. Dodd checked out a .38 pistol and strip searched the inmate, putting on a full set of chains. Their car took them right out on the tarmac

---

61 Murray at 112.

to the plane, where the pilot was standing. Since this was his first aircraft prisoner transport, Dodd asked the pilot where he could shoot on the plane. Without batting an eye, the pilot pointed at the engine and said, "Not there." Then the pilot pointed to the wing above his head and noted that it was full of fuel. Next the pilot pointed to his own seat and said, "Not there." Finally the pilot pointed to the rear of the plane and said that not much damage could be done by shooting toward the back of the plane. Dodd placed the cuffed inmate in the back of the plane, behind the pilot, and sat himself in a front seat. After transferring custody at the receiving jurisdiction, Dodd told the prisoner he would see him in a few months and the prisoner responded that he wouldn't see him again. True to his word, the prisoner escaped three weeks later and was killed at the shootout with police that followed.*

Blue Turner was a Lifer with a violent reputation. Lieutenant Dodd remembers the first time Turner appeared on his radar. A couple of weeks after a fire engine had been inside the prison yard for a fire, he watched as Turner burst through a door, then ran through the next door, locking it behind him. Following at a furious speed was another prisoner, brandishing a fireman's ax. The second prisoner was placed in segregation.*

In about 1975 Dodd was making his rounds with Officer Jimmy Hartford when he heard a loud bang and saw a cloud of smoke from the Lifers clubhouse. As Dodd entered the clubhouse, he saw Blue Turner beat a retreat through another exit and hustle toward the cell blocks. Dodd followed him to another prisoner's cell on F-tier. Dodd told him to stand for a shakedown, to which Turner tried to push past him on the walkway. Dodd took him down on the walkway and Officer Hartford nearly fell off the walkway to the very hard concrete many floors below in the ensuing scuffle. Dodd's search found two improvised shotguns in Turner's pants. The shotguns were made out of pipe, outfitted with a plumbing faucet turner that, when tightened, fired pellets. Turner was sent to segregation.*

34

Jobs I Worked and the Rat

At one time, I landed a job taking care of the lawn between six wing and the wall. It was nice to get away from all the prison hustle; no inmates could go there except me. I mowed the grass and planted flowers along the sidewalk, and it was a really nice gig.

Once I planted a batch of marigolds that hadn't bloomed yet, and the next day I found that they were gone. It turned out that a patrolling officer spotted them, pulled them up and took them to the control room, thinking he had found a garden of marijuana plants. His nickname from then on was Officer Marigold. Once you got a nickname in the joint, it tended to stay with you forever. When the officer couldn't take it anymore, he quit.

One day I found what at first appeared to be a large mouse. Over time, the young mouse turned into a beautiful black Norway rat, and we got along fine. I brought him treats and even made him a cage out of some bricks, complete with a wire mesh top. The rat and I were friends, and none of the officers bothered the rat, probably because they were afraid of getting an insulting nickname.

One day, Associate Warden Harvey decided my beautiful, black Norway rat must go. An officer went out to get the rat, but the rat refused to go, and the officer reported back without the rat. Next, Harvey sent the five-man prison guard goon squad to get the rat. They timed this so it happened just before the movie started in the theater.

The rat's cage was between six wing and Blood Alley, so a bunch of inmates stopped to see the goon squad try to capture the rat. They saw that once the rat was out of the cage, he started fighting back and actually charging the guards. The guards began trying to stomp on the rat and they were chasing him all around while the inmates all cheered for the rat and threatened officers if they killed the rat. Finally, one guard said, "F_____ it. Harvey can get his own f_____ing rat," and with that the rest of them all walked off. Just like that, the rat packed up and moved out of the area.

From my perspective Harvey's downfall happened because of his two big weaknesses:

1. He was a control freak so he would start a program and micromanage it, then start another and micromanage it, and this just kept building until finally he had all these programs that overextended his time, and then nothing was working right in the programs. He was stuck in the mud and eventually the higher-ups took notice.

2. He consorted with other corrections officer's wives and girlfriends.

Eventually Harvey got transferred to Shelton and started back into his old ways again, but this time I heard a guard there didn't want to share his wife or girlfriend with Harvey. As expected, Harvey was eventually shot in the face with the guard's shotgun, which didn't kill him but did make him quite unattractive to the ladies.

35

Pressure Punks and Businessman Ray

I remember one kid, in particular, who ended up a pressure punk.[62] This kid bought weed from a member of the BPFU and didn't pay his debt on-time. He owed something like $20 for some weed, so in prison currency that is $20 white money or $40 prison script, or 4 cartons of cigarettes. This was a substantial sum, so it wasn't surprising that there was some collection effort in the offing. His kiting checks in the mail for a couple of weeks had delayed his payments, and I guess he was feeling kind of cocky.

The penalty for not paying debts can be death, and it wasn't an unusual punishment for drug debtors. Lieutenant Dodd remembers an inmate who had his throat slit over a much larger amount: an $800 drug debt. When Dodd questioned why they would kill this debtor, knowing they would never get repaid, another inmate responded that it sent a powerful signal to all other debtors to pay up ASAP.* Of course, the same can be accomplished by killing a small-time debtor: once you whack a guy who owes a small amount of money, everyone else tends to catch up on their debts pretty quickly.

In this case the creditor had sold his debt to Ray. Ray was a good guy, but he had a weakness for young, scared white boys. More than one such boy gave up ass in the eight wing shower when Ray would tell him, "I want shit on my dick or blood on my shank." Once in a while a guy would say, "F____ you" and Ray would say, "Get the f___ out of here" and everything would be cool, with him and the other guy. Ray liked testing

---

62 The fact that I don't even remember his name gives you an idea of what fellow prisoners thought of pressure punks. They were the lowest of low, bottom of the barrel, least respected in the entire prison hierarchy.

135

them and it usually worked, though honestly the majority would take the dick and become a pressure punk.

As a businessman, Ray found around ten other guys who all paid Ray $5 to get some young, indebted, white boy's ass. Now no one is going to complain, not even the white guy, because, as a debtor, he broke inmate law and could have been killed according to that law. Not paying debts is punishable by death, and the punishment transfers to cellmates. If your cell partner gets indebted, you also can be killed according to the convict code, without any repercussions.[63]

To carry out the punishment, the kid was grabbed on the way to the movie and forced into the BPFU clubhouse. There he was forced to have sex with Ray and ten other guys.[64] When done, they threw him out into the breeze way, naked, so that everyone got the message. The message, of course, was that everyone needs to pay their drug bills, or risk being next. The reasons for the large, gang rapes were:

1. Ray, a savvy businessman, made his money back, and then some, for buying the bad debt;
2. There are 11 attackers that the kid would have to finger if he wanted revenge. This would result in a huge target on his back if the kid reported the rape;
3. The gang rape, while brutal, was really a kind gesture. According to the convict's code, the kid could have been murdered.
4. Because the kid could not seek revenge, he became a free game pressure punk. Anyone who wanted to have sex with him could. This extended the kid's punishment.

So, the kid's future looked pretty bleak, even hopeless. Then Blackie Palmer entered the picture and made it even darker. Blackie Palmer was an old-time convict who had been a con-boss for many years, before the break-up of the prison con-boss system. Blackie's name didn't describe his

---

63 Lots of things in prison under the convict code carried the death penalty, including stealing, not paying your debts and no minding your own business.
64 These things often happened in the clubhouses; except I don't remember it ever happening in the WSPMA (biker's) clubhouse.

complexion—he was white. It did, however, communicate his effect on others; Blackie was a small, wiry guy who liked to hurt people. He was a dark cloud to anyone's day.

Blackie Palmer liked kids, and so he moved the gang-raped kid into his cell in eight wing. Now the only one the kid had to have sex with was Blackie, and Blackie was older, so the kid only has to do it two or three times a week. Also, the kid understood that Blackie was not one to loan his kid out, unlike others, and this made the kid's life a little more bearable, if only for a while.

But Blackie had two weaknesses: drugs and kids, and it was drugs that proved to be his ultimate downfall. Blackie earned a good living selling drugs, but he didn't like paying taxes on his sales. The attitude in prison was that taxes were legitimate. Even the Bible said to give Caesar what is Caesar's. But being an old con-boss, Blackie despised the new system where he had to follow such rules. He wanted to go back to the old days where you had thirty to forty con-bosses running the joint, like it was their own country, not answering to anybody. Maybe Blackie had a third weakness in that he just couldn't accept change or adapt.

On December 23, 1975, he got a call from the RGC that his presence was requested at the RGC office during the 4:00 pm prison count. Prior to going to the office, Blackie checked with the eight wing guards on whom would attend this meeting. Since the meeting was during count time, the staff knew exactly who would be there, and I guess the names checked out with Blackie, because he went to the meeting.

I think ultimately Blackie agreed to go to the meeting for several reasons:

1. He was arrogant. Blackie was a tough con from the old school and thought he was untouchable;

2. He knew who would be at the meeting. It appeared prison-approved and well-planned, so he thought the meeting was going to be pretty straight-forward and businesslike;

3. He knew from guards that a free-world counselor named Mike

would be there. Blackie believed Mike would prevent anything bad from happening; and

4. He considered the three tax collectors attending the meeting of little risk to his safety, because they were so far beneath him.

So, off Blackie went to the RGC office, with bars on the windows and low ceilings, located in the old power plant. Immediately upon arrival, Blackie found three agitated, tax collecting inmates, baying for blood. The meeting "discussion", in which we can only assume that Blackie stood his ground on not paying taxes, turned violent. Blackie ended up meeting with a very violent end, with his blood staining the ceiling, walls, and floor.

Then the three tax collectors turned to Mike and informed him that he had not seen anything, which is really hard to imagine being true—the room was covered in blood and a man was dead. However, given the circumstances, Mike readily agreed that was the case.

Attempting to leave the RGC office, Mike collapsed outside the kitchen. He got up and ran to the control room, asking to be let out of the prison to the administration building. After getting into the administration building, Mike again collapsed, this time losing control of his bowels. Meanwhile, Mike spewed out details to the guards of Blackie's murder. So much for Mike's sworn oath of silence. Mike immediately quit his job as a free-world, do-gooder prison counselor, which can't surprise anyone. Next Blackie's son Dennis, also at Walla Walla, was moved to a Montana prison, since it was feared Dennis might be a target for spin-off violence.* I felt Dennis would have undoubtedly been killed had he remained in Walla Walla, given justice practices of the prisoners.

36

Prosecuting for Crimes Against Inmates

This should have been the world's easiest murder conviction. They rounded up the three inmates who slaughtered Blackie and placed them in segregation, charging them each with first-degree murder as well as violating the peace and dignity of the State of Washington. Arthur Eggers, the prosecuting attorney for Walla Walla County, assured the public that a conviction was imminent. With a free-world man as an eyewitness, the ability to place all five of them at the scene, and loads of forensic evidence, Eggers felt pretty confident.

Eggers diligently prepared his case against these three already-imprisoned perpetrators and was shocked when a jury of Walla Walla County Citizens failed to convict even one of the three. This verdict served the interests of Walla Walla residents just fine. They wouldn't break into a cold sweat every time the escape siren sounded, worried that an escapee was coming after them, because of a vote during a jury trial.

But to me, a prisoner, this marked the point when the entire town of Walla Walla sold out. At this jury verdict the town became bought into Connie's idea that the prison residents could and would govern themselves, and it was no longer a matter with which they would concern themselves. The county stopped caring about this poorly administrated, loosely-controlled, often very vulnerable prison population.

Shortly after Blackie was killed, his kid ended up dead. When word got out that three were arrested for Blackie's murder, someone thought Blackie's kid could finger all or one of the suspects and therefore, the kid must die. No one stopped to consider that the three alleged murderers already had tons of credible, eyewitness testimony against them. In the end, the kid was attacked in his cell by three prisoners and stabbed over 60 times.

Had the kid been a snitch, or even known anything about Blackie's murder to tell, the kid's murder might have sent a powerful message to any wannabe snitches. In the end, however, it was just another senseless prison murder. The three who killed Blackie's kid were also arrested and charged with first-degree murder, so Blackie Palmer's murder resulted in a total of six prisoner arrests with accompanying murder charges. The kid's murderers were tried and also found not guilty, once again demonstrating that the citizens of Walla Walla had washed their hands of any civic responsibility they might have in trying someone for a prisoner's death.

37

The Knife, aka Walter Carter

Walter was a young black man and a member of the BPFU. He'd gotten the nickname of The Knife, because he was always packing and quite often used what he was packing. In prison movies, knives are always something strange, like a toothbrush handle with a razor blade, or a 3-inch pen knife. To me, these are pretty laughable weapons; Hollywood doesn't spend a lot on research, apparently. Walter carried an 8-inch blade knife with a handle, and he knew how to use it.

One day, Walter decided to go to the control room to talk to Warden Rhay about transferring to the Minimum-Security Building or MSB. Rhay interviewed people with these requests, since he had the power to place an inmate anywhere, even over the objections of other prison staff. This process served to perpetuate prisoners' dreams that they could go to the farm, if only they could convince Warden Rhay that they wouldn't run off once they were there.

When you went into the waiting room to see Rhay, you were patted down. Once it was your turn to enter the conference room with Rhay, you were again patted down.

Walter was in the waiting room, getting patted down, but for some reason the guard had the door to the conference room opened while he was patting Walter down. Low and behold, the guard felt something in Walter's crotch area, besides the regular anatomical equipment. The guard told Walter to show the weapon and Walter pulled this big knife out. The guard disappeared, then was shortly replaced by a gang of guards. These guards took a look at the size of the knife and ran too. Warden Rhay saw the commotion and came out of his interview room with a .32-caliber automatic pistol in each hand. He told Walter, "Drop it, or I blow your brains out, you little punk." Walter quickly dropped the knife and was hauled off to segregation. I witnessed this event personally, as I was getting interviewed that same day. Shortly thereafter Walter was found dead and the BPFU club house was renamed Walter Carter Hall.

38

Bad News Harris

Bob Bad News Harris was a wino from the Wenatchee/Yakima orchards, serving time for murder. He got his name because it was known that if you messed with Bob, your family would read some bad news in the newspaper shortly.

One evening, Bad News was going through the chow line. Remember, in the chow hall, all the tables seated four and were bolted to the floor. Also remember, each table was owned by someone, so you had to ask permission to sit.

That evening the chain bus had dropped off a batch of new fish, all identifiable by their newcomer coveralls for the first week. The fish had been first through the chow line, and one of the fish was a big guy, making the unfortunate mistake of sitting at Bad News Harris' table. There was a bit of a hush as everyone in the chow hall picked up on this indiscretion. Everyone was on-alert, waiting to see what Bad News would do when he saw it. I didn't think Bad News was looking for trouble that day. I thought he just hoped the fish would be gone before he got through the chow line.

Well, this fish was a slow eater and was still at the table when Bad News showed up. Bad News told the fish that he was sitting at his table and needed to find his own table. This was generous of Bad News, it was a fair warning to a newcomer. All the fish had to say was, Oh, sorry. I didn't know it was your table, get up and move on; no one would have thought any less of him. But oh, no. This fish wanted to make a statement on his first day and he wanted to put Bad News in his place. So, the fish said really loud, This is my table now Pops. You can stand in the corner or eat on the floor.

Bad News threw down his tray and it shot toward the table. The fish jumped up with his fists ready to fight, while Bad News pulled out what looked like a tine off a tuning fork. By now there were three prison guards, standing close to the fish and Bad News. Two of the guards grabbed the fish. As soon as the guards grabbed the fish, Bad News stepped in. Bad News stabbed the fish in the heart and the fish dropped dead, right there in the chow hall on his first day at the prison. If you don't learn anything else, remember this: never let prison guards grab you if you're unarmed.

In the end, there were three prison guards standing within two feet of the complete crime scene. Also, at least 40 prisoners, all of whom relished the opportunity to testify against Bad News, also had a front-row seat to the action. I think every rat there put in a note to the administration, telling them what happened and that they would gladly testify about it.

It looked like there was no way that Bad News would get anything but the death penalty. But remember that the Walla Walla juries just didn't want to get involved with prison affairs. Since Connie's reforms, no jury had found a prisoner guilty of a murder. Months later the Walla Walla Union Bulletin headline reported that Harris was found not guilty by a jury. Having Ron McAdams as his defense attorney, a short but very good, Perry Mason-like lawyer, certainly helped. Bad News was also put on trial in the prison court, charged with inciting a riot. He was found not guilty there, because from a prisoner's perspective he was only protecting his property.

A little later I saw Bad News in an argument with one of his special kids. They ended up in front of the RGC office, where new grass had been planted and the area roped off with some stakes and string. Bad News slapped the kid and the kid pulled up one of the stakes. I watched as the kid swung the stake at Bad News. Next Bad News pulled out a shank and advanced toward the kid, and the kid started backing up. As he backed up, another stake that was tied by string to the first stake came out of the ground, then another came out of the ground. Eventually the kid had a stake in his hand that he was swinging at Bad News, while two stakes swung in the air, attached by string to the weaponized stake. The scene was, simultaneously, deadly serious and a hoot to watch.

Eventually the kid threw down the stakes, ripped his t-shirt open and said to Bad News, "Kill me! Just kill me!" I watched as Bad News put his shank away, the guard in Six Tower that had observed the whole thing lowered his rifle, and Bad News hugged the kid with the kid hugging him back, crying all the time. Everyone watching took a deep breath and watched as the loving couple was reunited.

Some prison guards were more willing to step into dangerous situations than others. Lieutenant Dodd remembers that the quicker you were to respond to an officer in need, the quicker others were to step in and help you. In about 1975 the inmate store was broken into. Dodd and four other officers responded, finding a crowd of prisoners all trying to get in on the looting. Dodd was gently bulldogging his way into the crowd when he heard Sgt Talbott yell, "623007 Curtis Johnson coming up behind you!" Dodd turned around to see 623007 sneaking up behind him, ready to strike. When Dodd made eye contact with the inmate, the inmate slunk off.*

Once Dodd was standing with a relatively new officer when one inmate asked the new officer, "Aren't you the officer that was standing on the breezeway when those two inmates were fighting? I saw you take off the other way." The new officer said, "Yes, that was me. Anytime I see fights, I don't care who it is, I'm going the other way." Dodd made it clear to supervision that he would refuse to work with that officer if ever he was sent his way again. Dodd's theory of survival in Walla Walla was that if ever you expected trouble, or if you were looking for trouble (like during shakedowns), you chose the most dependable staff you could find to accompany you.*

Among the more reliable staff, Dodd found, were many women. The prison didn't hire female guards to control the male prisoners until 1973. The theory behind including women as guards was that they could search female visitors. With the change in policy, contact visitation allowed for a deluge of contraband in the prison. Dodd felt like there had always, so long as he worked there, been a need for female guards and was grateful that someone in charge finally noticed. Not only were they able to control and discipline male prisoners, they also exercised good judgement and proved highly dependable in difficult situations. Dodd laments that some staff never accepted them, although they proved every bit as capable as men in doing their jobs. In fact, Dodd found that prisoners seemed softened by their female guards, as they seemed to behave better around them.* Lieutenant Dodd's story is a lot like watching the 1998 movie *U.S. Marshals* with Tommy Lee Jones.

39

The Movie Panic

The theater was at the end of Blood Alley, past six wing, five wing, and four wing, as well as the BPFU clubhouse. When you started toward Blood Alley, the only way out was to come back up Blood Alley, or else go into a wing, the theater, or the BPFU clubhouse.

More than just bloody attacks happened in Blood Alley. Lots of bad stuff went on there. It was lined with peddlers selling their wares, including everything from fresh pruno, to home-rolled cigarettes, to girls looking for a movie date. Some girls dated in 15-minute blocks, while others dated for the duration of the movie. If there were any guards in this area, it was only for briefly. Two guards walked down Blood Alley to open the theater, and then went into the theater, locking themselves in the theater's cage for protection while the movie played.

That night there was trouble, which was not uncommon. You haven't seen anger until you've seen a girl who got a $5 bill, only to discover it was a $1 bill with $5 edges. The trouble that night was different and more serious than usual: a revenge beating took place. Like all legitimate revenge beatings, this one required review, approval and scheduling.

To give some background, Jack Anderson was one of only three black men ever to be a member of the Bike Shop, and he asked permission to teach a rat a lesson. Bob Wentz, a serial rapist from Spokane County, ratted on Jack's kid, who was at the farm. The kid came in every night to go to his class in the education building. This made an excellent opportunity to bring in drugs, or so it was alleged. Bob tipped the guards that Jack's kid was bringing in drugs, and the kid lost his place at the farm, run back inside the prison walls. This cost Jack quite a lot of money, because now his business was gone. He worked hard to get this business together and now, because of a rat rapo, his lifelong hope of being an independent businessman was dashed; Jack and his kid were in prison again, and Jack was broke. To add insult to injury, good old Bob, a no-good rat, was living the good life at the farm. There had to be some trouble over this.

The Secret Police learned that the Good Right Reverend Smith (who was never right about anything, nor particularly good) was helping Bob's wife get through the difficulty of living alone. He was helping her water the grass and flowers, and in a number of other ways as well. A phone tap (by the Secret Police) revealed these goings-on and a girlfriend of someone did a little surveillance. It was discovered that every Thursday night the Reverend had a sleepover at Bob's wife's house. Thursday must have been particularly stressful for Bob's wife, and she needed extra help to get through it.

Bob was tipped off and freaked out. It was strange how a rapo could be so upset, because his wife was receiving a little divine help. Hadn't this man been taking that help by force just recently? But somehow, in Bob's mind, a line was crossed. The trap was set, and the cheese had been taken; everyone knew that Bob wasn't the kind of guy to let this just slide. We knew Bob was coming back from the farm, and some planned on then serving him his just desserts for ratting.

Bob decided to escape from the farm by sneaking out a window the night he was tipped as to the situation between his wife and Reverend Smith. It wasn't hard escaping--on the farm you are on-your-honor, after all. Bob left, heading for his wife's house on a Thursday night, and the reverend was there. Bob found the information was correct: Reverend Smith was assisting Bob's wife, as was his practice. Bob burst into the house during the middle of the help session and the reverend ran out, stopping at the first phone booth he found to call the cops. Once again Bob was back behind prison walls.

For being a hard-core serial rapist, Bob was not the smartest boy in town; he never realized that the whole thing was part of a ploy to get him back on the inside, so he could be punished. He should have PC'd up. Instead Bob came out of segregation (punishment for his escape) and took back his old job in the control room, typing memos for the cops. Meanwhile, the plan for Bob's revenge beating moved forward like clockwork. A movie night was planned. It was known that if the theater was showing a XXX movie, Bob always attended; "The Devil and Mrs. Jones" was just too much of a temptation.

When Jack came to the Bike Shop and asked if he could take care of Bob, the Rat Rapo, the prisoner's code said that he could take care of such matters by himself. So, Jack gave his kid a three-foot section of chain and instructed the kid to teach Bob a lesson about ratting.

In the theater, Bob was sitting in the row between the Bike Shop section and the BPFU, along with some other rapos. That was like a no-man's zone between the two powers' turf. During a particularly interesting segment of the movie, Jack's kid leapt up and started wailing on Bob with the chain. Bob had been caught with his pants down, literally, because he was messing with his squirrel. He couldn't run very well with his pants down. He did manage, however, to climb over a row of seats and into the BPFU section of the theater, all the while screaming while his blood was flying.

Later, after talking to some of the BPFU folks, I learned that the BPFU thought the Bike Shop was launching an attack. This would have violated the Treaty of 1973, which decreed that neither club would launch an attack in the theater. In a panic, the BPFU members rushed toward the front of the theater and up onto the stage. This building had an orchestra pit right in front of the stage. When the stage got full, BPFU members fell into the orchestra pit, which was about a 12-foot drop. Broken bones resulted.

In the meantime, the guards also panicked. The theater had a two-way light switch, with one of the guards upstairs in the projection room, sidetracked by the little games that the projection staff engaged in while the movie was running. Some staff members enjoyed the XXX-rated movies alongside the inmates and more than just Bob was caught with his pants down.

The theater grew particularly chaotic when one guard would hit the two-way light switch "on" and then, as if on cue, another would hit the switch off in another part of the theater, resulting in the lights only coming on for a second or two. It was truly wild. I saw George Smith, who worked in the electrical shop and liked to rat on folks, down in the aisle with someone jumping on top of him.

The seats were made out of pressed plywood, like many theater seats of the day, and they were quite strong. During one of the brief illuminated moments, I saw a BPFU member running toward the Bike Shop section and he ran *through* a seat; the seat exploded like it was made of cardboard. Talk about adrenalin pumping!

The theater's exit door was built such that only one person at a time could go through, so this large crowd surged to the door, trying to exit, with the crowd literally pushing people through the door. The old-timers sat in the first row of seats and the crowd that rushed the door pushed into their section, snapping the cast iron supports of the chairs and just about cutting the butt cheeks off of one old guy.

Finally, the lights came on for good and in the Bike Shop section there stood Bill Jackson, Carly Wilson, Blinky, and me, as well as non-Bike-Shop members Stanley, David Riel, and James Fogle. Many were not aware of the planned revenge beating, and they speculated that a bomb had gone off.

Bob went into protective custody, and the next movie in the theater was not well-attended. A few months later, an inmate went into Bob's cell and checked him for hemorrhoids. At Walla Walla, there really was no safe place for rats to hide.

40

The Riots

In the old days, the riots were handled quickly, without debate. When seven wing rioted in the 1960s, Warden Rhay raced to the wing with a 30-30 lever action rifle, firing one shot down the tier to get everyone's attention. The riot started quickly and ended just as fast. Late 60s, two inmates stormed the door, with hostages, going outside the walls to the Administration building, B.J. Rhay grabbed a .38 caliber revolver from the security booth and fired all six shots into the sally port. Both inmates surrendered. With the change in prisoner governance, things changed.

The first big riot of the 1970s occurred in 1974 and involved taking the hospital.[65] A group of inmates stormed the prison hospital, which was three stories tall; on the main floor were medical procedures, on the second floor were the hospital beds, and on the third floor were the dings, with Dr. Hunter in charge. When the mob broke into the main floor, they were first distracted by the pharmacy and the promise of drugs. Windows were broken and drugs were thrown to the waiting crowd outside the hospital. The staff, under direction of Warden Rhay, sat back, not knowing what to do. Connie had made it plain that the prison was to be run by inmates, while the staff's job was merely to see that no inmate left before his time was served. Warden Rhay decided to call the RGC leadership and see what could be done to restore order.

Now a debate was on between the RGC members and the staff. Question one was whether this was just a simple protest gone wrong—could the situation be handled without the RGC looking like stool

---

65 Murray at 93.

151

pigeons? The debate continued, with the guards just standing there, waiting for orders.

In the meanwhile, rioters were trying to gain access to the second floor of the hospital, and there was talk of killing some snitches housed on the third floor. Inmates on the second floor wouldn't allow rioters access, which put their lives at serious risk. One inmate managed to take two second-floor nurses hostage.

Talk did arise that maybe a couple of the female nurses could be used for entertainment purposes by the prisoners. One inmate, who worked as an EMT, held the would-be rapos off with a jar of alcohol and a Bunsen burner. Finally, the staff decided to lockdown the prison and continue negotiating with the rioters.

Prisoners got word from the RGC that the negotiations would continue. All inmates needed to stay locked down, no matter what the guards allowed. That meant that even if the guards opened your cell, no one could come out of his cell until told to do so by the RGC. If a prisoner broke this inmate-initiated lockdown, he could easily get issued an RGC death penalty.

Unfortunately for the prisoners, lockdown meant that inmate meals, three times a day, were prepared by staff. This was costly for the institution and very unappetizing for the prisoners. Morning and evening meals were TV dinners, and lunch was only a sack lunch. Overweight prisoners lost weight under these conditions, amidst much wailing and gnashing of teeth.

Lockdown dealt consequences besides meal disruption. This riot occurred before television was allowed, so boredom was a huge problem. Some cell partners were beaten, others were raped, and it was not a good time for prisoners or staff.

Back at the hospital the RGC determined that it was not a riot, but rather a protest, and that the prisoners responsible would not be punished when they came out. Of course, the staff wanted none of that, so the lockdown continued, and the rioters retained their hold of the prison hospital's main floor. Finally, Washington's Department Social and Health Services stepped in and concurred that it was not a riot, but rather a simple protest, and promised that if the inmates themselves would discipline the instigators, no punishment would result. The hospital was turned back to the staff and two days later the RGC called off the lockdown.

Eight wing had another riot in the late 1970s, though this time a warden did not fire shots into the wing. Once again a lockdown was called and negotiations between staff and the RGC commenced. This time it was a bit more serious, because a few inmates wanted to kill or rape a guard who was trapped in the wing. Luckily for the guard, some inmates gave him refuge and his murder and/or rape was stopped. Ironically, later on this officer killed another off-duty guard.[66]

In November 1976, Washington elected its first Democrat in twelve years as governor: Dixy Lee Ray. Her campaign platform included removing adult corrections from the Department of Social and Health Services and creating a separate department, which didn't actually happen until 1981. In the meanwhile, Governor Ray put Harlan McNutt, an old friend and psychiatrist, as Director of Department of Social and Health Services, and McNutt made Douglas Vinzant Warden Rhay's replacement for warden in June 1977.

Things got pretty crazy under Vinzant. If the life of prisoners was pretty free before, it only got better, at least for those prisoners in power. Vinzant removed any restrictions on clothing. Now the queens wore makeup, skirts and blouses.[67] Prisoners could come and go throughout the day within the prison walls, from breakfast to lockup. Girls would come in from Whitman College and hang out all day. One prisoner said, It was pretty much, do what you wanna do, just don't let me see you killing nobody or beating nobody up or don't let me see you trying to escape . . . As long as you did your time, they didn't care.[68]

The problem was that longstanding rules, usually unwritten, were no longer observed by prisoners. The strong dominated the weak, and the wannabes reinforced the culture. Personal property was no longer safe. Older, vulnerable men were sometimes victimized by those with greater

66 Murray at 221-26.
67 Murray at 152.
68 Murray at 145.

strength and fewer scruples. Small wrongs brought disproportionate responses. The leaders led, the followers followed, and the victims suffered.[69]
The only tool at prisoner disposal for rule enforcement was violence, so
that is how discipline was maintained by the clubs. This gave prisoners in
power something they really wanted to protect: the status quo.

Lieutenant Dodd remembers well the years with Superintendent
Vinzant and Associate of Custody Genakos. According to Dodd, there
was nothing good to be said about Vinzant and Genakos.* Among their
various shortcomings as administrators, they were known to pay prisoners
for information.* Not only was this illegal, but it also cost many prisoners their lives.* When Vinzant and Genakos arrived at Washington State
Prison, Dodd was a new lieutenant working relief. Immediately Dodd
was called into Genakos' office, told he wasn't a team player, and put on
nights, which lasted three long months.

Dodd was once unknowingly party to Vinzant and Genakos' strange
dealings with inmates. One night at about 1:00 am, Vinzant called from
the warden's house. Dodd was instructed to leave two inmates in the RGC
office after 2:00 am, which was when the last of the outcount inmates in
the RGC office were supposed to be locked up. Dodd asked how he was
supposed to just leave these inmates, without raising the suspicions of the
other prisoners and confusing the two left-behinds. He was told that the
two inmates already knew, and they would just hang behind.

Then at 2:00 am Vinzant called Dodd again and told him to get
the kitchen keys and meet Vinzant with the two convicts at the kitchen
entrance. About 15 minutes later Vinzant and Genakos arrived at the
kitchen door. They told Dodd to let them and the two convicts into the
kitchen, and then wait outside. About five minutes later they came out
of the kitchen with a cloth sack about the size of a pillowcase. They told
Dodd to take the inmates to the control room and then come out to the
superintendent's office.

When Dodd got there, Vinzant and Genakos told Dodd to call a
corrections officer in from home, check out a car, and then deliver the

---

69 Murray at 151.

two inmates to the Washington State Reformatory. He did so, delivering the inmates at 8:00 am to their new home. He was never told what was in the bag and he never saw those two inmates again. After another prison lieutenant gave Vinzant and Genakos his unvarnished, negative opinion on how they were running the prison, Dodd was no longer top of their shit list and was returned to days.*

On August 12, 1978, Lieutenant Dodd remembers being off-duty when his phone rang at 4:30 am. He was ordered to report immediately to work, no questions asked. It turned out that at around 3:00 am Lieutenant Roger Sanders, a usually overly-cautious guard, found an inmate-produced pipe bomb. He proceeded to try to take it apart and, in the process, it blew up, killing him and injuring two other guards. After this explosion, Vinzant and Genakos resigned.* The staff union played a role in securing their resignations.*

41

Warden James Spalding

Warden James C. Spalding started at the prison in the late 1960s. His father had been a captain at Deer Lodge, a Montana prison, so he had a pretty broad prison background. He started at Walla Walla as a guard and was soon promoted to sergeant. He was a sergeant when I entered Walla Walla in February 1972. Jim had a brother named Mike, who also worked as a prison guard there, and Mike had been exposed to Agent Orange while in Vietnam. Mike Spalding and I seemed to have a lot in common, with our Vietnam service, and Mike didn't really like being a prison guard, but it was a family tradition for him.

I later fell out of favor with Mike, due to his brother's dislike for me.[70] My first error was that I ordained Mike as a pastor in the Universal Life Church, after which we had a little ceremony. James Spalding was not impressed. My second error was at a prison court, where I was called as a witness against Little Dave, who was charged with attempted escape. Spalding didn't appreciate my testimony at the trial when I swore that I had not seen Little Dave on the evening in question. James Spalding told me right after court that he would get even with me.

Spalding was made warden in August of 1978, taking over after Vinzant was fired (or resigned, or whatever).[71] When Spalding took control the

---

70 I requested the Minimum-Security Building—Farm (MSB) twice, and Spalding turned me down the first time. The second time I applied was in the fall of 1979. Spalding was on leave with a back problem and Father James Cummings was acting superintendent at the time. Cummings cleared me for the MSB and when Spalding returned, he let the ruling stand.
71 Murray at 184.

incident involving the pipe bomb had just taken place. From the beginning, Spalding put in place security improvements, making the prison more secure for guards. He found that the inmates "owned" everything. "In effect, the administration didn't own anything inside that facility. It was just operating at the whim of the inmates."[72]

This didn't set well with the bike shop. Spalding did two things that hit the bike shop pretty hard. First, he quit letting prisoners go out into the community. We used to be able to take a corrections officer and use inmate welfare funds to go into the community for a few days. Second, he took the bike shop clubhouse from the main institution and put it in the industries area, causing a decline in club membership and influence.[73]

We in the bike shop felt wronged, because our club was doing good things. We didn't cost anything, because we did our own fundraising. We taught skills to prisoners, who could then use those skills when released, and our club's leadership reduced violence in the prison.[74] Once our club's influence waned, we weren't able to keep as much control, and violence increased, with lots of knifings and small riots.

Spalding's solution was to move the prison leadership to "the farm".[75] Meanwhile, he was trying to clean up the prison by making structural changes to the facility, which gave lots of folks trying to protect the status quo an incentive to resist the changes. At the time, the CTI was at war (again) with the Chicano club, and the CTI was getting the worse of the feud. Because several members had been killed or stabbed, the majority of the CTI started packing shanks. All this didn't cause any concern to the Bike Shop, because bike shop members were off-limits to these attacks.

---

72 Murray at 186.
73 Murray at 189.
74 Murray at 190.
75 Murray at 198.

Warden James Spalding.
Photo by Ethan Hoffman.

Sgt. Bill Cross. His death ended the great experiment.
He was stabbed to death outside the South Dining Hall at the Walls.
Photo supplied by James Spalding, Director of Corrections.

One day, in June 1979 a CTI member came out of the chow hall where the doors were only a half a block from Six Tower Gate, a gun tower with a clear shot at the kitchen. Sergeant Billy Cross decided to step forward and do a pat down search of the CTI member after no one on his staff offered to do the search. His staff were behaving prudently; it turned out that the tribal member told Sergeant Cross that he was packing and to just let him go. Instead, Sergeant Cross insisted on disarming the member, and in the process, was stabbed to death in clear sight of the tower and in front of hundreds of inmates. I look back and see that this marked a turning point:

victims of prison violence changed from prisoners to staff.[76] I suppose it was inevitable that Spalding looked to transition from prisoner self-governance, to a return as a staff-run institution.

Sergeant Cross's stabbing spurred a dash to the cell blocks by a lot of inmates, for all knew that serious violence could occur if the staff abandoned the prison. Like me, a lot of prisoners had made preparations for self-preservation in case of an uncontrolled riot. Prisoners had chains to lock their cell doors shut, along with lances equipped with shanks, and some even had fire extinguishers. Several hours after Cross died the staff managed to convince the inmates, who hadn't already returned to their cells, to go there.

This photo of Governor Ray was taken in front of the Chow Hall. In May of 1978 a year later in June 1979 Sgt. Bill Cross will be killed where Governor Ray stands in this photo
Photo supplied by James Spalding, Director of Corrections.

76 Murray at 208.0

42

Lockdown, the Punishment that Keeps on Giving

I felt that Sergeant Cross was a good guy and didn't deserve to die this way, but I saw things from a different perspective than Spalding. It seemed like Spalding was making prison violence worse rather than better. Instead of backing off, Spalding kept on pushing as he tried to wrest control from the prison clubs. This was July and a rat named George was working the mechanical room in eight wing. This rat turned off the air conditioning, with all the inmates on lockdown, just to inflict misery on the cell block. Most of the guards just didn't care.

During this lockdown, violence started as a trickle and then accelerated. At first there was a lot of trash thrown down, occasionally after being lit on fire. The cell block was three tiers high with each tier connected by stairs, with six rows of cells, two on each tier, and just a handrail on the walkway for the upper tiers. Many a young prisoner had been thrown off the upper tiers into the abyss below. Bike shop members lived on A tier, one of the bottom tiers.

One third-floor prisoner, believed to be a guy named Harpo, located on the bike shop side of the cell block decided to plug his running sink and toilet, thereby flooding his cell. Other prisoners liked how the water cascading down looked and joined in. Then a guard, without asking anyone, decided to turn off the water to the cell block.

Still on lockdown in un-airconditioned cells, inmate rage boiled over. Among the inmates, word came down that everyone should destroy all their sinks and toilets, which was easy to do since they were porcelain.

In the end the guard's decision to turn off the water led to an entire cell block's destruction.

The staff had to decide what to do next. It became obvious that the prisoners could not be housed in a cellblock without plumbing. During summer of 1979, they moved all of us from eight wing to outside. The Big Yard, which was a three- to five-acre outdoor exercise area, became our new home. It was large enough to have a full-sized baseball diamond but had no bathrooms and just one drinking fountain. They called in the state patrol to move inmates out of their cells after dark. Rations were limited: each of us got a blanket as we were escorted into the Big Yard.

With no bathrooms and no shade, the Big Yard was a harsh solution, in my opinion. I saw many inmates collapse from sunstroke. Administration brought in two porta-potties (what choice did they have?), though they sawed off the top with a chain saw, so again there was no shade from the sun. Quickly we learned that two porta-potties were just not enough for 350 men. Two hours after they were brought in, you would have to take a shit by standing against the sides of the porta-potty, which inside already had a pile of shit three feet above the toilet seat.

They solved the problem of too few porta-potties by having them serviced twice a day. Since we got to see him so much, we quickly realized the porta-pottie guy was in a league of his own. When he came in, the prison guards and Highway Patrol ordered all of us to the other side of the yard. Their drawn guns encouraged compliance with this order. The way-too-cool guy from Ned's Service then came in and sucked the toilets out with his shitsucking machine. On one occasion Ned, the Shitsucker, was holding the hose with one hand and eating a sandwich with the other. Shit didn't bother Ned any.

Following the inmate power hierarchy, the more powerful inmates took blankets from the less powerful inmates so that tents could be made. The days were hot and the nights really cold, yet some inmates never had a blanket, much less a tent.

This arrangement continued for 30 days while they worked on repairing the cell block. At the end of 30 days, on August 1, eight wing had already been re-plumbed with one-piece stainless steel sinks and toilets.

We moved back into the cell block, only two to a cell. Our beds were now bolted to the walls, and the wiring, ventilation system, and shatterproof windows were all improvements from the past.

Since all the cells were now identical, there was no longer a market for "renting" cells.[77] Even though we were back in our cells, we remained on modified lockdown throughout the summer. We could leave our cells if a visitor came, and we got to shower and have clean clothes and bedding. Some prisoners got to exercise, and a few inmates returned to work in the license plate factory. Even classes at the education building resumed, but mostly we were still locked in our cells, with lock down meals. We had a cold breakfast in the morning and TV dinners twice a day, every single day.[78]

Meanwhile the prison staff was suffering from severe mayhem. They were trying to crack down on contraband and it took a lot of searching. Lieutenant Dodd remembers supervising a crew assigned to clear six wing of all contraband. Another crew had eight wing, which he remembers as a flooded-out mess. The fruits of this cell clearing resulted in 33 dump trucks of trash, all found in the cells. Personal property was boxed and sent to the property room, and extra state linens, as well as mattresses, were returned to the laundry.*

On October 12, 1979, attorneys representing inmates filed Hoptowit v. Ray in federal court.[79] The Ninth Circuit Court of Appeals had already ruled that incarceration in the Washington State Penitentiary was cruel and unusual punishment due to poor lighting and other hazardous conditions;[80] certainly losing the cellblock's plumbing would not improve their opinion of the facility.

Finally, around a week later and four months after it began, the lockdown ended. People's Park, where there used to be green grass, was covered in concrete. The prison had beefed-up officer manning and prisoners weren't allowed to loiter anywhere, except in the Big Yard. The club

---

77 Murray at 242-243.
78 Murray at 243.
79 682 P. 2d 1237 (9th Cir. 1981).
80 Hoptowit v. Spellman 753 P.2d 779, 784 (9th Cir. 1985)

areas were common turf, and no area belonged to any group of prisoners anymore. Now the prison staff ran the inmate store. There was a strict gate system in-place that kept prisoners locked in their cells, locked in a double-guarded dayroom or rec area, or working at their jobs.[81]

The Hoptowit case wasn't over. Instead it ping-ponged up and down the federal court system. Ultimately the 9th Circuit found that the lack of security for inmates at Walla Walla violated a number of protections, including the US Constitution's protection from "cruel and unusual punishment."[82]

During this time, all the club houses were closed, and the prisoners ate in staggered shifts; gone were the days of the guys in six wing eating with the guys in eight wing. For the first time in twelve years, a week went by without a stabbing, and a month went by without a killing. The administration finally took back their prison.

Though Dr. Conte resigned as Director of the Department of Institutions in 1971, his ideas were alive and well for many years. When Spalding took charge in late 1978, this changed. Spalding was pretty fair in my estimation, but at the time, he did not care for me and I felt likewise.

---

81 Murray at 246.
82 Hoptowit v. Ray, 682 F 2d 1237 (9th Cir, 1985); Hoptowit v. Spellman, 753 F. 2d 779 (9th Cir, 1988).

43

Minimum Security

Prisoners were always trying to get assigned to the Minimum-Security Building (MSB or The Farm), possibly because there was less violence there. However, while I was there from December 1979 to March 1981, the building saw its first killing.

If someone got tired of living at the MSB, he could go ask to get back inside the prison or he could escape, oftentimes just by just walking away. Many who escaped would be gone only a week or so and then be back. One black guy named Todd disappeared and was not immediately caught. Rumors developed that he was dead and buried out on the farm somewhere. In fact, he was captured months later.

I put in for the The Farm twice. Spalding turned me down the first time. The second time, in the fall of 1979, I applied while he was on leave for a back problem. Father James Cummings was Acting Superintendent , and the good father cleared me for the MSB; when Spalding returned, he let the ruling stand. This allowed me to spend my last year or so of prison at The Farm.

When Father Cummings first came to the prison, he came from Ireland and was hired as the Catholic Priest for the prison. His first paycheck was for $900-plus and he stormed into Warden Rhay's office, announcing that there was no way he would work for that kind of money. He thought they had paid him in full for a year of work. It was explained that every month he would get a check for that amount, which appeased him. The good father, it was said, was too fond of the hard drink.

When I got to the MSB, I was assigned to the motor pool since I had taught auto mechanics for two years at the prison college. The motor pool did all the maintenance for the prison's fleet of vehicles, and even worked on the Warden's and Associate Warden's cars, as well as occasionally their children's cars.

When I got there, the motor pool was run by one of the old con-bosses, who had been there a long time and thought he was a free world man; in truth, he was still an inmate. In just two months, I was in full control of the motor pool and hired only Bike Shop members, who were people I could trust to do things right. The motor pool became so efficient that other state institutions started sending their vehicles to the prison for repairs. This caught Spalding's attention and finally my checkered past was forgiven.

Following my 1971 conviction, I appealed various elements of the trial, none of which were successful. Next were pleas to the parole board, which also proved unsuccessful. In spite of my lack of success in the courts and before the parole board, the case continued to make headlines in the local paper. It seemed like every year the case would reappear on the front page of the *Walla Walla Union Bulletin*. One year it was a $3000 reward for new evidence, then another year a story featuring retired officials talking about how the investigation was mismanaged and how the evidence didn't support the conviction. Finally, nearly a decade later, there was a headline, reporting that the governor had released me from prison.

What eventually got me out of prison was a circumstance out of my control, seemingly random. In 1980, Washington's governor Dixy Lee Ray was conducting a random tour and inspection of the Washington State Patrol Training Academy, where they were using the investigation into Pam's death as an example of how *not* to investigate a crime. After hearing the discussion, Governor Ray had the compassion and insight to question what had happened to the convicted husband in that case, and academy personnel admitted that I was still in prison. Governor Ray, in October 1980, commuted my, and seven other prisoners', life sentences. All of us were convicted based on scant, unfairly prejudicial, and generally unconstitutionally-admitted evidence. In other words, Governor Ray could see that I had been railroaded by investigators, as had the other men. In October 1980, Spalding called me into his office to announce that the governor had ordered me released.

Between October and my release, the following spring, Jim called me in his office to ask if, once released, I would come back and run the motor pool as a free world man. I thanked him for the offer, but declined. I'd had enough of the Washington State Penitentiary.

Governor Dixy Lee Ray tours the Walls in 1978.
Photo supplied by James Spalding, Director of Corrections.

Conclusion

My actual release didn't come until March 1981. After what I had been through it shouldn't have surprised me that it would take six months for the state to process my release paperwork. While getting my life together after release in summer 1981, I got a call from Spalding, who was then Director of Corrections for Washington. He asked me to do him a favor and call Amos Reed, the director of Washington's Department of Social and Health Services, and I agreed.

Amos Reed was an interesting man. He talked with a Southern accent like Sheriff Andy on *The Andy Griffith Show* and he would really beat around the bush, never speaking directly. Mr. Reed offered me a position in treatment at the Washington State Penitentiary. His reasons were that I had training in psychology and was respected by both guards and inmates. At first, I was overwhelmed and thought that would be a great opportunity to help those I had left behind in prison.

So, my first thought was yes, and I almost took the job. In the position I would work directly for Jim Spalding, who worked out of Olympia. Then, almost as a second thought, Amos said, "We got us one little hangnail son that you're going to have to handle right off. You see them bikers, bless their hearts, still have the motorcycles out in the industrial area. They need to leave that area." I explained to him that the bikes weren't just motorcycles to those bikers, but they were a part of their souls. I told him that if you rip someone's soul away, there will be trouble.

Then I got to see the other side of Amos. He said, "Son, those f---ing motorcycles are going. You're going to get rid of them now; first thing, ya hear me clear?" I told him that I could not accept the position. I reported back to Spalding that the offer was interesting, but I would not and could not accept it, and warned Spalding that moving the bikes, no matter how tight their security, would spark a bad reaction.

During summer 1981, after the prison administration took back power from the inmates, and after I was gone, officials decided that the bikes were a symbol of Bike Shop power. Even though the Bike Shop no longer had a dedicated meeting place, and their power in the prison was no longer absolute, they still had their bikes in the industries area. The announcement regarding removal of the bikes was made over the Washington State Prison TV channel, a month after I had turned down Amos' offer. A few days later the dining hall and kitchen went up in flames during an inmate riot. I might add that there is no proof that any Bike Shop member had a hand in the destruction of the dining hall.

As typically occurs after a riot, the prison went into lockdown and all the prisoners were searched. Various kitchen knives and shanks were discovered and, early in the lockdown, a plan was developed to get rid of the bikes.

The owner of each bike was identified and given tools and his bike. The prisoner-owner was to dismantle his bike and put the parts in the box. The box was then shipped to an address chosen by the biker. If a bike was unclaimed, it went into storage. This marked the end of Bike Club power at the Washington State Penitentiary[83].

A little later, I got another call from Spalding, asking me to call Amos again, which I did. He was all nicey-nice, using that southern charm and said they were looking for someone to run the prison motor pool and my name came highly recommended. I had seen the other side of Amos and had talked to others who had seen that side, and once again I turned down the offer. That was the last I heard from Amos.

In 1994 Spalding called me. I don't know how he tracked me down, but he wanted to invite me to a seminar he was speaking at in Spokane. I accepted the invitation and afterwards talked with him over dinner for several hours. He told me I did the right thing when I turned down the

83 Murray, pp. 264-5.

offer of working in treatment, stating that Amos was impossible to work for.

In hindsight, after that decade of prison terror, I realized how fortunate I was to finally find some justice in my release and vowed I would clear my name. I learned a lot over the previous few years and knew I needed a really good criminal lawyer, one who was respected by the courts. I settled on Mark Volves from Spokane, who said he would need $10,000 on retainer to take my case. I started saving money, which was difficult given that I was starting all over in making a career for myself. Finally, in 1994 I had the money.

In December 1996 the trial court in Walla Walla County heard our petition for a new trial. Many witnesses were called, including Larry Kinchloe, the former warden at Walla Walla and then current warden of Alaska's penitentiary. My lawyer called me to the stand, and I testified for quite a while, then it was the prosecutor's turn to question me. I still remember as though it was yesterday that the state's attorney told the court that the state had no questions for the defendant. The judge asked him again and the attorney confirmed that they had no questions for me. The entire packed courtroom was deadly quiet, as they felt the gravity of what had just occurred. The judge then announced he would make a decision then and there. The judge did not find that a new trial be called, because of the lack of evidence. The state agreed and then the judge ordered a not guilty verdict be entered into the record. For me that was the moment where the ordeal truly ended.

Exonerated, I was able to find jobs in auto and motorcycle shops, eventually owning my own motorcycle parts distribution company. I married and had another child, a daughter, who with her life, gave me a new life, a vision of something grand that my life could become.

Phillip Daniels: States Star Witness

To Suspect

On May 23rd, 1980 Michael Prager reported in the Walla Walla Union Bulletin page 2, the following:

During the trial of Kelley Messinger, Phillip Daniels had testified that on the night of Mrs. Messinger death he had a date with her and was going to pick her up "at the Red Apple Restaurant about the time it was determined Mrs. Messinger died." Michael Prager, Reporter for the WWUB.

Daniels testified in Court that he did not keep his date with Mrs. Messinger that night.

"Gary Williams, now a resident of California, states in the affidavit he was told by a trial witness a story different than the testimony given by the witness at the trial. Williams states in the affidavit that Daniels told him the opposite story --- that Daniels did meet her. The conversation took place after the murder, when Daniels, Williams and two other friends were driving around town, Williams states." Michael Prager, Reporter WWUB.

Convicted murderer requests new trial

By MICHAEL PRAGER
Of the Union Bulletin

Kelley Messinger, convicted in November 1971 of first-degree murder in the strangulation slaying of his 16-year-old wife, is asking for a new trial.

Messinger, who's been serving a life sentence at the state prison here since his conviction, claims that new evidence contained in a December 1979 affidavit could reverse his conviction.

A motion for a new trial has been filed with Division Three of the Washington Court of Appeals at Spokane.

The motion is based on new testimony supplied by a former Walla Walla resident and an acquaintance of Messinger's at the time of the murder.

Gary Williams, now a resident of California, states in the affidavit he was told by a trial witness a story different than the testimony given by the witness at the trial.

According to trial testimony, Mrs. Messinger had arranged a meeting with a friend, Phil Daniels, at the Red Apple Restaurant about the time it was determined Mrs. Messinger died.

Daniels testified the meeting with Mrs. Messinger never took place as arranged. Williams states in the affidavit that Daniels told him the opposite story — that Daniels did meet her. The conversation took place after the murder, when Daniels, Williams and two other friends were driving around town, Williams states.

Credit: Walla Walla Union Bulletin. Used by permission.

Deviant Behavior

Prepared for the Governor of the State of Washington,
at the request of the Governor
Governor, Dixie Lee Ray

Under the Direction of James Spalding Superintendent,
Washington State Penitentiary

Written by Kelley D. Messinger

The belief that deviants are different is built upon a series of false assumptions because all deviant behavior is human behavior and the basic processes for producing behavior are the same for a deviant as for a non-deviant as these persons fundamentally have the same essential components, but this concept does leave way for further considerations:

Biology and Social Behavior

There are no physical functions or structures, no combination of genes, and no glandular secretions which contain in themselves the power to guide, direct, or determine the type, form and source of social behavior of human social behavior. Despite this, there are still some scientists who believe that certain types of deviant behavior can be traced to certain physical anomalies or to heredity. There have been explanations in terms of body type, glandular troubles, brain pathology and the relation of chromosomes to deviant behavior, particularly in the area of crime which is a theory that fascinates me. Some biologists believe that crime, alcoholism, certain types of mental illness, and certain types of sexual deviation can be carried as specific unit factors in biological inheritance in much the same manner as eye color or hair color is inherited through the genes. Such theories as this have been found invalid because there are to many variables and too many accepted concepts to the contrary. It is feasible through that behavioral traits can be passed on in the family through the sharing of common experiences and attitudes.

Physical defects like crossed eyes, facial deformities, acne and other deformities are thought by some to have relation to certain forms of deviancy and crime. Due to negative societal reaction, persons with physical defects of these types are often more likely to be processed and labeled as deviants by authorities and find their way into some type of institution. A physical handicap of this nature may cause a person indirectly to seek certain contacts which could lead to deviant behavior.

A group in which a person orientates his behavior to is called a reference group.

Although people get their attitudes from their culture and from sub-culture situations, occasionally attitudes result from some type of unique personal experience. Like a person who has the police beat him brutally will develop a disrespect or hatred towards law enforcement and the police. Research on attitudes has brought out the fact that they can and do change. It is important through to distinguish between compliance as behavior change and attitude change. Outward behavior is changed more often than internally held attitudes. For instance, a person may comply by the rules in a prison situation but hold the same attitudes he had towards crime when that person is released as the person had before he was arrested.

Experimental research has concluded that the greater the reward for a type of behavior, the less there is a change in attitude. Some of the important variables which change attitudes are:

1. The strength of a particular attitude in the presence of external influences.
2. Increased familiarity due to firsthand experience.
3. The prestige of the model presenting a given attitude.

Even motives are acquired as the result of social experience. They are socially molded in accordance with the norms of groups to which the individual belongs. In the process of reaching goals, deviants and non-deviants may adopt what appears to be a different pattern of behavior, but they may be achieving similar goals in their own ways.

Self and Identity

Students of human behavior have come to recognize the importance of personal identity, for what a person does or does not do depends in a large measure upon the persons conception of their self. By virtue of being who they are, they assume status in a group. A person can locate themselves and is recognized by others, and their relationship to each of the others is thereby defined. Human behavior consists of a succession of adjustments to like conditions, but each person must come to terms with their self as well as with other features of their world. To understand what people, do, we must know something about what each person means to themselves. No hard and fast lines can be drawn between ourselves and selves of others since our own selves exist only insofar as the selves of others exist. The dynamics of deviant behavior cannot be understood without understanding the relation between deviance and self-identity.

The self is a set of discrete roles and identities which require both the responses of others and the acceptance of such designations by the actor themselves. They must sort out the meaning of what is happening to them in terms of their conception of who they really are. This requires the ability to distinguish between doing and being, for the self-motivated deviant commits deviant acts as part of the conscious process of becoming deviant.

Socialization and Social Roles:

Social behavior is not present at birth, it is learned and develops through socialization. Practically all behavior is a product of social interaction and is seen only in relation to other people.

Both deviants and non-deviants play a variety of social roles which represent the behavior that is expected of a person in each position or status with reference to a given group. A person's social roles are linked with their position or status in society, and each of these has role prescriptions. There are age roles, sex roles, family roles, and occupational roles.

Although a great deal of socialization in role-playing and role-taking occurs in childhood, it also continues into later life as people learn new roles and abandon old ones as they pass through the life cycle and encounter new situations.

A social role involves four parts:

1. An identification of self
2. Behavior in each situation appropriate to this identification
3. A background of related acts by others (COUNTER ROLES) which serve as rules to guide specific performance
4. The evaluation by the individual and by others, of the role enactments.

The required behavior, habits, beliefs, attitudes, and motives are an individual's prescribed roles. The requirements themselves are the role prescriptions. The role prescriptions are learned on interaction with others. What roles a child learns in the family and elsewhere are largely dictated by society itself. Groups then, are systems of roles and a group is what its' roles relations are. The role relationships within a group represent the ways in which its' members adapt to their relationships with each other. Much deviant behavior then is directly expressive of roles. The diversity of social roles is an important factor in the extent of social deviation in modern society. So, one can speak of deviant roles in the same way of any other roles as much of deviant behavior is motivated by an expression of roles. There are several reasons for viewing deviant behavior in terms of roles. Here are some of them:

1. It brings diverse actions together into a particular category or style of life.
2. A deviant role provides a meaningfulness to interactive situations, the meanings being assigned based on imputed self and other roles.

3. Deviant social roles make it possible for the observer or the public to reduce diverse behavior to a simple stereotype version of the role.
4. The deviant develops a self-conception through selective identification with the deviant role out of the many roles he plays.

When other people come to stress a particular deviant role a person plays, it is difficult for this person not to regard his deviance essential to his identity. The status and role which a person is assigned cannot be easily changed by his own desires whether a person plays the role society has assigned them or not, their behavior is still often interpreted by society as consistent with this role and its' corresponding status. For instance, a criminal returning to society that is making a legitimate effort to go straight may, be being interpreted by society as a person with a criminal status and role, give in and play the role expected of him.

Primary and Secondary Deviants

Based on social roles, deviants can be distinguished as either primary or secondary deviants. The secondary deviant being a career deviant. People can engage in deviant acts and still occupy a conventional status and role. This type of deviant behavior constitutes primary deviance when it is rationalized and considered as a function of a socially acceptable role. If deviant acts do not materially affect the persons self-concept, or give them a deviant role, they remain primary. Secondary deviance develops when the deviant role is reinforced through participation with other more pronounced deviants with whom the individual comes to associate with, and often through the effects of labeling. For instance, like a drug user that becomes more and deeper involved in a drug sub-culture and thus moving into an organized deviant group. Deviant groups tend to be pushed into rationalizing their position. Then when a deviant enters a group, they learn how to go on with their deviant activity with a minimum of trouble. Thus, the deviant who enters an organized deviant group is more likely than before to continue in deviant activity because they have learned how to avoid trouble and developed a rationale for continuing. Through a combination of socialization into the role and the development of appropriate rationalizations, they positively value their deviant role and status. There is also the concept of labeling. Labeling a person as a deviant my result in a self-fulfilling prophecy because a person labeled deviant, may continue in acts of deviance, and become a secondary deviant.

The following steps point out how one is led by official labeling and relabeling from primary to secondary deviance.

1. Primary deviation.
2. Social penalties.
3. Further primary deviation
4. Stronger penalties and rejection.
5. Further deviation, perhaps with hostilities and resentment beginning to focus upon those doing the penalizing.
6. Crisis reached in the tolerant quotient, expressed in formal action by the community stigmatizing of the deviant.
7. Strengthening of the deviant conduct as a negative reaction to the stigmatizing penalties.
8. Ultimate acceptance of deviant social status and efforts at adjustment based on the associated roles.

    Official labeling does influence behavior in many cases. Society often stigmatizes a person not so much for having committed a crime, but because they have been convicted of a felony or sent to prison. Although labeling is not a necessary condition for all secondary deviants, it is likely to be the case in some instances. Though the offender may not react at all, or they may deny the act or rationalize it away. They might even repeat the act or label themselves as deviant. On the labeling aspect, there also is some evidence that labeling may terminate deviance by its' effect on self-identity.

9. The more time a person serves the more likely they are to reoffend.

Deviant Acts

Most deviant acts do not just happen, they develop over a period of time out of process or a series of stages. Some deviant acts, like vandalism often begin without the person intending to commit the act, but the act builds up interaction with others.

The direction of a deviant act depends not only on past experience and learning, but also on the responses of others to the situation, for it is these responses of others which the individual takes into account in defining the situation and which they organize into their own behavior. In many cases, unanticipated consequences arise from events which were not even considered in the earlier stages of the deviant act.

Many deviant acts require some kind of physical artifacts for their commission. These artifacts are referred to as "hardware". For instance, for a robber to commit the deviant act of armed robbery, they will need a knife or a gun. This would be their hardware. Deviant acts are countless, and branch into a variety of cultures and sub-cultures among people from all walks of life.

To become a person engaged in deviant behavior it is a learning process. To pull one out of the cycle of engaging in deviant behavior is also a learning process. The answer and the only answer to stopping the deviant behavioral cycle is College level education nothing else will work.

Recidivism Rate

After arriving at the Washington State Petitionary in 1971 I was assigned by the job's placement Lieutenant to the inside prison control room, at the order of the Superintendent B.J. Rhay my job Control Room Coordinator. I over saw three other inmates and they typed up all the orders of the day and miscellaneous memos. Why did I get this job? It was explained to me by A.J Crowley Associate Superintendent of Custody that B.J. wanted to know where I was always, since it was believed I had been a member of the Weather Underground (Weathermen) and served in the ONI (Office of Naval Intelligence) and trained in jungle warfare, making me an extreme escape risk in the staff's eyes. None of it was true but once put, in a Memo, it was certain fact.

It was while working in this position that I became aware of how many men left and then came back in a short period of time to start another sentence for a new crime or for a parole violation which could be issued with or without cause.

To discover the cause of this became my daily quest when time allowed. Quickly I discovered that an Inmate who stayed out of trouble in prison was just as likely to return as a troublemaker. So, it was obvious that getting a third off your sentence for being good in prison changed nothing on the outside as far as behavior went.

Further I observed that the inmates who were involved in the self-help movements, Lifers with Hope, Awareness group or any program run by the inmates made no difference in changing a person's rate of success once released. Maybe committing crimes is a mental illness of a sort, so how do we fix that. While cooling my heels in Shelton, the DOC Receiving/

Classification Unit which decided where an Inmate would do their time. I got a book from the library on Psychology and quickly concluded that to stop the return rate, therapy is what we needed. Once arriving at the Washington State Penitentiary, I continued to read books on therapy treatment.

Dr. Beck the founder of CBT (Cognitive Behavior Therapy) recognized that many of the troubled in life can be given the skills to change their behavior using CBI (Cognitive Behavior Intervention).

It was obvious that forced therapy was not the answer, oh they would go and excel in a passive aggressive behavioral manner. You can make me go but, I will not listen or learn attitude.

So why had the great prison reform of the 60s and 70s failed so badly?

1. We assumed that if a program worked in Europe it would work in the USA, but it did not.
2. The people in Europe were let us say dogs and the inmates were wolves both canines. In the USA, the people are dogs, but the inmates are like cats. You cannot train them. They have to be motivated then they will change themselves.
3. The Staff in charge of the Washington State Penitentiary during the late 60s and 70s did not get involved in the program, instead they just threw it out there and let some inmates try to sort it out.
4. Repour was the other problem, this program needs someone who is respected by the Guards, the Staff and the Inmates. This individual was never found, because no one cared to look for the right person to lead this new experiment.

Being in the Bike Shop leadership, I was pretty much aware of what was going on in the prison at any given time. We had this new threat arise in the B.P.F.U. An inmate just off of Death Row named Tony Wheat, was a three-time murder. My first induction with Tony was in People's Park, he was speaking and when finished held up his clinched fist and shouted Black Power and the crowd loved it. I decided (Bike Shop) we needed to keep an eye on Tony. It was during this period that something strange started happening with Tony. He started to mellow out, the clinched fist was gone, he was still in leadership in the B.P.F.U. and was a remarkably effective leader. So, what had changed with Tony in the last year? He started taking advantage of the Education Program that was offered but looked down upon by most of the inmates, a place rats and child molesters went.

This caught my attention and I started going to school to track the progress of those involved in the program, and after a few years was astounded with what I had discovered.

- The Inmate who received a GED was 45% more likely to excel once being released
- The Inmate who received an AA degree was 61% more likely to excel once being released.
- The Inmate who received an BA degree was 74% more likely to excel once being released.

When we educated Inmates by primary offering Alcohol & Drug classes, Psychology and Sociology classes, we achieved the goals sought in CBI therapy and the students were not even aware they were being treated!

Tony Wheat is the poster child for my suggestion of treatment. Mad dog killer, Revolutionary to a free man who will not reoffend and will be an asset to our society. In 1968 no one would have thought this possible, society at that time thought the answer was to kill him via the death penalty.

What does this Educational Treatment do for our Society?

1. When these Inmates return home, they are most likely going to be the first college graduate from their family.
2. Now the younger brother now has a different example to follow. His older brother has moved on not hanging with the old homies.
3. When a man has 4 children and he has a 4-year degree, guess what happens? Three of those children will also go to college instead of stealing cars and etcetera.
4. The downside DOC loses their customer base.

This cycle can be broken. In the late 70s, Superintendent Spalding called me into his office and told me, "Governor Ray wants a report on what causes Deviant Behavior, I want you to write it." What happened, Governor Ray lost her party's nomination and the practices at DOC have not changed in all those years.

We know the answer now and we can change these Inmates' lives, by incentivizing them to go to school. How, simply change the good time rule. You now get a third off your sentence, (or hopefully more) by satisfactorily completing the educational programs offered by DOC. This will also change our society not just an Inmates life. We can turn the convicted into productive law-abiding citizens.

The following articles came from the
Walla Walla Union Bulletin.

WW man graduates cum laude at prison

By MICHAEL PRAGER
Of the Union Bulletin

In 1971, Walla Wallan Kelley Messinger was convicted of murder and sent to the state prison. Friday he graduated cum laude from Washington State University's prison education program.

Messinger was among 211 inmates receiving degrees and certificates in ceremonies in the prison's outdoor visiting area.

"Education opens so many doors," Messinger said after receiving his bachelor's degree with a 3.82 grade average. "It makes one's world bigger."

During his nine years at the prison, Messinger, 33, also has earned associate degrees in academic studies and auto mechanics. Education is a good way to kill time and stay out of trouble while in prison, he said, adding he's never been "tagged" for an institutional infraction.

But he has spent a lot of time appealing his first-degree murder conviction from Walla Walla County for the strangulation slaying of his 16-year-old wife in August, 1970.

Messinger, a former postman, is pinning hopes for release on a recently filed affidavit, pointing to new evidence in the case. He is asking the state Court of Appeals for a new trial.

Since his conviction in November 1971, Messinger has lost all of his appeals. But he steadfastly maintains his innocence.

Messinger a McLoughlin Union High School graduate, hopes to be released by the courts soon so he can put to work the degree he earned Friday.

"Education is a very important program in this prison," he said.

Commencement speaker Leonard Jackson, a former inmate, told the graduates that his education at prison was the single most important factor in his success at staying out of prison.

Jackson, who said he served three prison terms, was released last year and works now in Pendleton as an alcohol and drug counselor for the Umatilla Indian tribe.

"When I was in prison last time, I made some decisions I was going to go in a different direction," Jackson said.

He encouraged inmate graduates to "think positive. Say to yourself, 'I am somebody.'

"If you do, people in the community will see the same thing."

In all, eight bachelor's degrees were awarded, including one to a graduate of The Evergreen State College, Michael Finnegan. It is the first time an inmate has

KELLEY MESSINGER: Graduates cum laude at prison

received a degree from Evergreen.

Other WSU graduates are Richard Ashbaugh, Robert Harris, John Haverty, William Newman, Tommie Stewart and Timothy Williams.

Eric Gabrielsen, academic education coordinator, said that despite the prison's turbulent year, education programs proved productive.

Walla Walla Community College awarded associate degrees in academics and vocational studies, including welding, auto mechanics, barbering, office machine repair, upholstery, welding and engineering technology.

Eighty-four inmates received high-school completion degrees. One-year certificates were awarded in drafting and custodial service.

"Some of these fellows never did anything in their lives," said Jim Cummins, associate superintendent of custody. This is a real accomplishment for them."

Messinger noted after the ceremony that during his college studies, he completed a survey on recidivism of prison education graduates.

Of those receiving two years of education, the return rate to prison was 39 percent during the past seven years. Those with four years education had a 19 percent return rate. The return rate for inmates without education is about 80 percent, Messinger said.

From the article, 10th-13th paragraphs:

Commencement speaker Leonard Jackson, a former inmate, told the graduates that his education at prison was the single most important factor in his success at staying out of prison.

Jackson, who said he served three prison terms, was released last year and work now in Pendleton as an alcohol and drug counselor for the Umatilla Indian tribe.

"When I was in prison last time. I made some decisions I was going to go in a different direction" Jackson said.

He encouraged inmate graduates to think positive. Say to yourself, 'I am somebody.'

If you do, people in the community will see the same thing."

From the article, last two paragraphs:

Messinger noted after the ceremony that during his college studies, he completed a survey on recidivism of prison education graduates.

Of those receiving two years of education, the return rate to prison was 39 percent during the past seven years. Those with four years education had a 19 percent return rate. The return rate for inmates without education is about 80 percent. Messinger said.

Henry Liebmann

Walla Walla County Coroner for 8 years.

Henry Liebmann served with the Walla Walla Police Department and the Walla Walla County Sheriff's Department for an additional 24 years.

Declares MESSINGER innocent.

"They convicted Kelley Messinger without one sherd of evidence."

As reported in the Walla Walla Union Bulletin, May 7, 1979, page 11 as reported by Vance Orchard.

From the article (right), near the end:

"Then, there was another murder case where it was just the opposite, The husband was accused of smothering his wife to death, then throwing her nude body out alongside a country road.

"They never did produce a shred of evidence that he had committed the crimes.

"Yet they found him guilty."

Henry Liebmann with mementos from over 30 years of law enforcement work

He 'backed into' police work — and stayed

By VANCE ORCHARD
Of the Union-Bulletin

When Henry P. Liebmann, 75, 417 Balm St., retired last year as Walla Walla County Coroner he completed a career in police investigative work spanning more than 30 years.

His last eight years as coroner came on top of 24 years with the Walla Walla Police and Walla Walla County Sheriff's Department.

Liebmann started his career in law enforcement "late in life" in 1947, when he somewhat reluctantly took a job as a police officer here.

While he might have "backed into" the job, at a time when jobs were scarce, Liebmann has never regretted the decision he made as a 43-year-old man with no previous law enforcement experience.

Liebmann at the time was closing out a job as an airplane mechanic at the World War II Army Air Corps

our senior citizens

base here (now the Walla Walla County-City Airport).

"I was one of the last employees there; the summer of 1946 there were no longer any airplanes at the base," he says.

"That fall, I took the exam for police officer; I thought it would be an 'across-the-hole' when I was looking for work.

"In January, 1947, Capt. Ed Kanz called me in and said the position was open and offered it to me that I refused, saying 'I'd try to find something else.'

"In March, he called me in again and said he'd have to take me off the eligibility list if I didn't take the job then. So, not having lined up a job yet, I decided to become a policeman."

When Liebmann started duties as a Walla Walla Police officer, the town was even more difficult coming at 42, Liebmann says.

"There are many things about police work that are different than other work and a most important one is the need for a team effort that one has the gall," he says.

Reflecting back on the three careers in police work, Liebmann has some advice for those in that work today.

"In this respect, I was real fortunate.

"Chief Jefferis told me at the outset: 'Every man has problems and it isn't every wife who can stand having a husband in police work' — the dangers and the odd hours — the job is very demanding and even more demanding in many ways on the wife than on the individual policeman."

In the late 1940s, before the mechanization of farming, huge "armies" of transient laborers flocked into Walla Walla for the peas and grain harvests.

"The trouble was, there was no place for them to stay as there is today, so those men just hung around the taverns downtown.

"The biggest 'jungle' was from Mullan Avenue to the Walla Walla Gardeners' Association, along Mill Creek starting where the Walla Walla Coop is now.

"There was another at the north end of Second Avenue where the overpass is now.

"They were vagrants and often were jailed for this offense.

"Then, the farmers would come to the police station and bawl us out for jailing their workers.

"By paying the bail, usually about $5, the farmers could take whatever number of workers they needed.

"In 1950 they put me in plain clothes to work the taverns. The town was in an uproar over juveniles drinking in taverns then.

"About that time, I passed the exam for sergeant and made it, along with two others of the eight who took it: Don Wood (now Assistant Police Chief Wood) and Bill Keene.

"I never went back to uniform."

For 15 years on the police force, Liebmann was in the detective division.

"It's a lot harder job today than it was then," he says.

After 18½ years on the police force here Liebmann was named chief criminal deputy for the Walla Walla County Sheriff's Department.

He served there until 1969, when he retired at 63.

The retirement lasted two weeks, when he accepted the appointment as Walla Walla County Coroner, when former Washington State Patrol detachment chief Loy Kennedy died.

"Law enforcement people wanted me to take the job," he says. He filled out the year left of Kennedy's term, then was elected to two more 4-year terms."

"No policeman or detective is a hero; he is only as good as his informants and only as good as the information passed between one law enforcement person and another.

"If a policeman today thinks he's going to go out there and be the sole man on the force and solve all the crimes, he's a fool!

"The more cooperation you can get between law enforcement agencies the better. If you have the police department fighting the sheriff's office or the state patrol fighting the police department you're just defeating the whole program.

"One little bit of information can be the key to solving a big case, but if the policeman keeps that to himself, then it's too bad."

Liebmann feels combining elements of law enforcement agen-

cies could be an excellent way of saving the taxpayer money.

"I've always believed there is a lot of duplication that could be combined, such as the records office, communications, and the jail facilities.

"There's no reason those things couldn't be combined.

"They could be in the same building; I've always felt there should be that setup.

"But, you can't take them up; you can't take a policeman off the streets of Walla Walla and send him out to Burbank or Eureka.

"Or, vice versa for the sheriff's office."

Liebmann accepted the job of coroner because law enforcement people felt a man served in crime investigation was best suited for the task, he says.

"An ideal coroner would be somebody with law enforcement training and who was also a forensic pathologist.

"If you had to take one or the other, it would be more important to pick the one with the law enforcement experience."

During his nearly nine years as coroner in Walla Walla County, what did he recall as memorable cases?

"I'd say the one which proved the most disappointing was the case where a woman was found murdered. The police work on the case was real good; it looked like an 'open-and-shut' case if you ever saw one. In my book, I couldn't see how the case could be lost.

"And yet, the jury turned the ac-cused loose.

"Then, there was another murder

case here where it was just the opposite. The husband was accused of smothering his wife to death, then throwing her nude body out alongside a country road.

"They never did produce a shred of evidence that he had committed the crime.

"Yet, the jury found him guilty."

Liebmann says of his coroner career: "I enjoyed the work, though, even if it did mean lots of times being routed out of bed at 3 a.m. to go to the scene of an accident or worse."

Liebmann and his wife, Sylvia, are ardent collectors of pottery, an interesting hobby they have pursued for several years.

The couple has three children, Dauna Walster, Milton-Freewater; Patricia Moore, Walla Walla, and Sharon Philipp of Willingboro, N.J.

193

Woman agrees man innocent

To the editor:

I was deeply bothered by the May 7 article about Mr. Liebmann. Anyone who has been in the Walla Walla area for any length of time is aware of the Messinger case which Mr. Liebmann commented on.

I must also agree with him when he said, "They never did produce a shred of evidence that he had committed the crime." That's been almost nine years ago. I think this wrong should be righted. Nine years behind bars on that kind of evidence is a miscarriage of justice!

Cathleen M. Campbell
West 1826 Gardner
Spokane

From a letter to the editor:

Woman agrees man innocent

To the editor:

I was deeply bothered by the May 7 article about Mr. Liebmann. Anyone who has been in the Walla Walla area for any length of time is aware of the Messinger case which Mr. Liebmann commented on.

I must also agree with him when he said. They never did produce a shred of evidence that he had committed the crime." That's been almost nine years ago. I think this wrong should be righted. Nine years behind bars on that kind of evidence is a miscarriage of justice.

Bike Shop banquet in the Big Yard.
Photo supplied by James Spalding, Director of Corrections.

Bike Shop banquet in the Big Yard.
Photo supplied by James Spalding, Director of Corrections.

Bike Shop banquet in the Big Yard.
Photo supplied by James Spalding, Director of Corrections.

Bike Shop banquet in the Big Yard.
Photo supplied by James Spalding, Director of Corrections.

Bike Shop banquet in the Big Yard.
Photo supplied by James Spalding, Director of Corrections.

Bike Shop banquet in the Big Yard.
Photo supplied by James Spalding, Director of Corrections.

Chopper in the Big Yard at the Walls.
Photo supplied by James Spalding, Director of Corrections.

Glossary of Prison Terms

Ace of Spades: You're going to get hurt or killed soon, better check in to protective custody, punk.

Baby Raper: Child molester.

Beef: A crime in which you were convicted.

Boom Box: A large radio.

BPFU: Black Prisoners Forum Unlimited

Breezeway Bum: Guy who would sit in the breezeway all day. Many were snitches.

Breezeway Commando: A wannabe tough guy who prowls the breezeways looking for an easy victim. Could be a robbery or just an easy sexual encounter.

Bro: A brother in crime.

Bum Beef: Guy who says he is not guilty. Not many denied to the population that they really had a bum beef.

Chain: A bunch of Fish coming into the prison.

Cheese Breath: He's got cheese on his breath; He's been ratting on people

Chipping Bitch: Guy who would have an affair on her man.

Con/Convict: A person serving time who has a nutsack. Not everyone serving time will be a convict or con.

Con-wise: A person who gets no infractions because he doesn't break the rules. A reason for the parole board to reject his Good Time.

Cops/Coppers/Bull/Guard/Pigs/The Man: All words for a correctional officer.

Count: Counting the inmates 3 to 4 times a day to insure no one left without permission.

Crank: Another word for speed or Meth.

Ding: A crazy person not quite right in the head, doing strange unpredictable behavior.

Do-Gooder: A free world person who is blind to what is going on, but thinks he can help everyone.

Doper: Drug addict.

Dr. Mengele: When you get to the third floor, tell Dr. Mengele (A German Nazi doctor who performed deadly human experiments on prisoners and was a member of the team of doctors who selected victims to be killed in the gas chambers in World War II) hello. Another name for Dr. Hunter who ran the unit until the 9th District Circuit Court closed the unit down.

Dry Snitch: Guy who leaves out evidence so someone will get caught by the cops, i.e. Snitch says to a Bull: You might want to check out A Tier.

Farm: The minimum security building located outside of the walls.

Finger Wave: Getting your anus checked out by a guard's finger.

Fish: New guy to the prison.

Free World Man: A person working inside the walls who is not a correctional officer.

Get Down: To Fight with fists or weapons, i.e. Let's get down then!!

Girl: A guy who dresses and acts like a girl.

Glue Sniffer: Guy who gets high sniffing glue.

Good Time: You get a third off your sentence if you obey the rules.

Heart: He has heart, he will fight to the end.

Holding the Bag: Someone who is holding a bunch of drugs.

Hole: Segregation cells, also known as Big Red.

Home Boy: A guy from your home town.

Inmate: The new word for a person doing time.

Jacket: Inmates personnel file showing all infractions, etc.

Jailhouse Lawyer: Guy who goes to the law library and writes writs. One court action in King County was to free primates in the zoo for unlawful imprisonment

Kiester Stash: Hiding things in your anal cavity.

Kite: A form sent in to the staff for an interview with a staff member.

Making a Play: Trying to get a favor you are not entitled to; being deceptive.

Mary Jane: Marijuana

Mule: Someone who smuggles drugs into the prison.

Nickel Bag: Five dollars worth of marijuana.

Nutsack: Got balls, will fight if pushed.

Off: Kill someone, to off them.

Outfit: A device to shoot up some drugs.

Pat Down: To be searched without having to take off your clothes

Pink Kid: Looking young and fresh. Sometimes called a Cherry

Point Man: A guy who is looking for the Bulls while a crime is being committed.

Popped: Got arrested

Pressure Punk: Guy who is forced or pressured to be a girl in prison.

Program: Go to school, get in a self-help group. Something to impress the parole board with.

Protective Custody/PC: Inmates segregated from the general prison population for their safety, i.e. Going up in PC in Five Wing.

Pruno: Homemade wine, generally made out of split peas: Potent and cheap. Can also be made out of canned fruit: Potent, but expensive.

Punk: A low life, a weasel, a want-to-be.

Pussy: Weak-ass punk with no nutsack. A girl's anus.

Queen: Another word for girl, but generally a queen would be more likely to sell her favors.

Rack the Cells: Lever used to close all the doors on the tier at once. To tier a section of prison cells.

Rapo: Rapist.

Rat Pack: More than one inmate would assault another inmate.

Reefer: A marijuana cigarette.

Resident: Newer name for a person doing time.

RGC: Residential Governmental Council. The self governing arm of the prison. Made up of influential inmates.

Script: Prison printed money. Often the inmates would print counterfeit script.

Shank: A homemade knife.

Shine On: Make little of the threat.

Shive: A homemade knife.

Skin Search: Inmate who is searched by taking off ALL of their clothing. Often done in public.

Smack: Another word for Heroin.

Snitch Jacket: A person who was known to be a rat.

Snitch Kite: Writing down an infraction and sending it to a guard without signing it.

Snitch/Rat: Guy who informs on people to get time off or accommodations; Cheese eater.

Snitched Off: Snitch/tell on another inmate.

Speed: Old term for Meth.

Speed Freak: Drug user who prefers Meth.

Square John: An inmate who is not a criminal and knows nothing about what he is getting into.

Stick: To stab with a shank

Stool Pigeon: Another word for a rat.

Streets: The world outside the prison.

Tag: An infraction of prison rules when written up is referred to as a tag.

The Shop: Washington State Penitentiary Motorcycle Association.

Third Floor: The mental health unit. Also called the Ding Wing Shop.

Tree Jumper : A Rapo who would jump out of a tree onto his victim

Wacky Tobaccy: Marijuana.

Wantabe: A guy who visions himself a tough guy, but is not tough enough to get into any of the real hard-core clubs. Might dress like a biker, etc.

Weed: Marijuana/Pot/Dope/Smoke/Reefer.

White Money: U.S. Currency.

Yard: Prison ball field.

If you got searched by Lt. Dodd, you didn't have to worry about him finding
something on you that was not there when you left your cell. You may not
have liked the Lt. but he was a straight shooter and would not allow the staff to
corrupt him. His bravery was admired by officers and inmates alike. He turned
the Goon Squad into the Dodd Squad. Interstate Tommy, a member of the
Bike Shop, pinned Dodd Squad on the Lt.

On one occasion while Jim (James Spalding, Director of Corrections) was
running the Idaho Department of Corrections, I asked him, "Do you miss
anything at Walla Walla?" He replied, "Yes, the Dodd Squad."